ention

Jh

Housing Design

Crime Prevention Through Housing Design

Edited by Paul Stollard

Principal of Rosborough Stollard,
Architectural Technologists
and
lecturer at the Queen's University of Belfast

E & F N SPON
An imprint of Chapman & Hall
LONDON • NEW YORK • TOKYO • MELBOURNE • MADRAS

UK   Chapman and Hall, 2–6 Boundary Row, London SE1 8HN

USA   Van Nostrand Reinhold, 115 5th Avenue, New York NY10003

JAPAN   Chapman and Hall Japan, Thomson Publishing Japan,
            Hirakawacho Nemoto Building, 7F, 1-7-11 Hirakawa-cho,
            Chiyoda-ku, Tokyo 102

AUSTRALIA   Chapman and Hall Australia, Thomas Nelson Australia,
            102 Dodds Street, South Melbourne, Victoria 3205

INDIA   Chapman and Hall India, R. Seshadri, 32 Second Main Road,
            CIT East, Madras 600 035

First edition 1991

© 1991 Paul Stollard

Typeset in 10½/12½pt Times by Scarborough Typesetting
Services, Scarborough
Printed in Great Britain by T. J. Press (Padstow) Ltd, Padstow,
Cornwall

ISBN 0 419 15370 5
     0 442 31317 9(USA)

British Library Cataloguing in Publication Data
Crime prevention through housing design.
   1. Great Britain. Residences. Burglary. Prevention.
   I. Stollard, P.
   364.4

ISBN 0–419–15370–5

Library of Congress Cataloging-in-Publication Data
Crime prevention through housing design / edited by P. Stollard.
   p. cm.
Includes bibliographical references and index.
ISBN 0-442-31317-9
1. Crime prevention and architectural design. 2. Architecture,
Domestic. I. Stollard, P. (Paul), 1956–
HV7431.C76 1991
364.4'9—dc20   90–41026
                                                    CIP

Contents

Contributors

Karen Croucher
Steve Osborn
Henry Shaftoe
Frances Warren

Illustrated by Karen Roberts

Preface

This book considers the potential for reducing crime and improving community safety through housing design. Guidance is provided for architects and planners on the process of assessing housing developments, considering alternative security strategies, developing the design and controlling the construction process. While every estate and neighbourhood has different problems and therefore requires a unique design solution, the process which leads to that solution will be the same. This book does not offer a precise set of guidelines, instead it attempts to outline the principles which architects and planners should consider during the process of assessment, design and construction.

Architects and planners should be designing to deter crime. Although it may not be possible to create a residential utopia, it should be possible to reduce the opportunities for crime and increase people's sense of security. However, designers must also be aware that attempted solutions to security problems do not have one single simple consequence. In fact some 'solutions' may make matters worse. The use of 'target-hardening' techniques such as security grilles and door reinforcements can create a 'fortress' which may provoke more ingenious or violent attacks. At the same time it can lead to an increase in the social isolation felt by the residents and reduce the fragile community support networks which are also such an important defence against crime. Architects and planners must aim for prevention rather than containment.

The text of this book has been compiled and updated from two working papers published by the Institute of Advanced Architectural Studies in 1988 and 1989. Chapters 2 and 7 are derived from *Safe as Houses* by Frances Warren and Paul Stollard, which looked at the layout of new housing developments. Chapters 4, 6 and 8 are mainly from *Safer Neighbourhoods* by Paul Stollard, Steve Osborn, Henry Shaftoe and Karen Croucher. This second working paper considered the process of improving existing housing estates to reduce crime and enhance community safety. The remaining three chapters combine parts of both working papers.

The first three chapters consider the underlying theories of the relationship between crime and design with reference to academic research work and recent publications. The final five chapters are concerned with the practice of crime prevention through housing design and are accompanied by suggested lists of further reading. As complete a bibliography as possible is also provided to all aspects of the problem at the end of the book.

1

Design and crime

In recent years many of the household surveys undertaken to gauge national and local opinions on social issues and the quality of life have identified 'crime' as one of the major concerns. Glasgow University's recent quality of life study (Rogers *et al.*, 1989) found that 'low levels of crime' was the most desirable environmental factor perceived by the general public. *The Second Islington Crime Survey* (Middlesex Polytechnic, 1990) found that in the three years since the first survey, crime had moved from third place to the top of the list of problems identified as affecting the neighbourhood. It was cited by 80.5% of people, compared with 71% in 1986.

The links between levels of crime and housing design have also been the subject of much discussion and research. When looking for simplistic answers to crime and social problems it has been easy to blame design without considering other factors such as the style of housing management, the mix of tenancies, local levels of unemployment and available social amenities. As yet there is no conclusive evidence to prove that design is the major factor in creating or solving problems of law and order. Design, on its own, does not cause crime or cause people to become criminals; however, some design features do appear to exacerbate local crime problems, although the same features in a different situation may not have the same effect.

1.1 FACTS ABOUT CRIME

Although crime, or the fear of crime, can have a dramatic and devastating effect on peoples' every day lives, the public often have an exaggerated and inaccurate perception of the true nature and level of crime. Architects, planners and housing managers must work together with residents and local communities to develop an accurate picture of what is happening and to try and identify why problems exist, before they can formulate solutions.

Before 1980 most of our information about crime came from official crime statistics, which included only those crimes reported to and recorded by the police. However, in recent years local and national crime surveys have greatly increased the amount of information available. Taken together, these surveys have shown that crime is more widespread than records previously showed: more than twice as much burglary, five times as many woundings and ten times as much vandalism.

However, the chances of being a victim remain slight. On average individuals are likely to be a victim of robbery (thefts or attempted thefts involving threats or actual force) once in every 200 years, of theft from the person (without threats or actual force) once in every 100 years and of wounding once in every 70 years. Households are likely to experience burglary (with loss) only once every 37 years, theft of vehicles once every 50 years, theft from motor vehicles once in every 9 years and vandalism once in every 6 years. Most crime is non-violent and involves property offences: most commonly thefts from motor vehicles, vandalism and burglary.

Much crime is carried out by young people and one half of all recorded crime is carried out by people under 21; nearly two-thirds of burglaries are carried out by people in this age group. The peak age for male convictions is 18 and for female convictions 15. Before their 28th birthday 30% of men have acquired a criminal conviction. Prior to 1988, the male peak was 15, but increasing use of police cautioning as opposed to charging has led to a reduction in juvenile convictions.

Crime is unevenly distributed across the country and throughout the population, being concentrated in inner urban areas and on large housing estates. Those that suffer most are the low-income households. On some high crime council estates, 1 in every 5 households is the victim of burglary each year, and a member of every 10 households is a victim of assault. Unskilled

Most crime is non-violent.

workers are twice as likely to be burgled as professional workers. Black people are more likely to be victims of crime than white and council tenants more than home owners. Young men are more likely to be victims of assault, although they tend to be the least fearful, while elderly people tend to be the most fearful and least likely to be victims. When sexual assault and domestic violence are taken into consideration, young women are more likely to be victims than young men. One quarter of reported violent crime involves domestic violence against women, and women and children are more likely to be attacked by someone they know in their home than by a stranger in the street.

Despite this picture of crime as an urban problem, the crime rate in certain parts of the suburbs has been rising at equal or even greater rates than in the city. Surveys show that there is considerable justification for focusing attention on inner city and outer urban estates, particularly in the most deprived areas. Yet it would be wrong to suppose that crime is a feature of only these areas or that crime in suburban areas or towns is insignificant.

1.2 FEAR OF CRIME

It is not only crime which is a problem, the fear of crime can be almost as serious in its consequences. Such fear cannot be dismissed solely as the result of media distortion of unreliable crime statistics and a focus on violent, but rare, crimes. For many people fear of crime is at least partly dependent on their own experience, such as witnessing acts of vandalism or knowing someone who has been a victim. For some, fear of crime also reflects the greater likelihood of becoming a victim. Women are generally more fearful of crime and also suffer more from certain types of crime, such as sexual assault, domestic violence and street robbery. Not surprisingly where crime rates are highest, people are more fearful. In many inner city areas, and on some outer council estates, significant numbers of people (women, elderly people and some ethnic groups in particular) are living in a state of considerable anxiety. Fear of crime causes those who can to move away from what are seen as crime prone areas and those who cannot to retreat into their homes. As a result, the control which the community itself can exert over antisocial or petty criminal behaviour is reduced.

The Second Islington Crime Survey rejects the argument that the fear of crime greatly exaggerates the real risks. It argues that the high levels of fear experienced by women are entirely rational. The survey found that 74% of women, as opposed to 40% of men, stay in fairly or very often. Not going out is cited as only the most extreme result of the fear of crime, other behaviour includes avoiding certain streets, people and public transport, or always having a male companion. The survey concludes that 26% of women aged 16–24, 27% of those aged 25–54 and 68% of those aged over 55 never go out alone at night.

Despite being much less at risk than other groups the fear of crime is particularly prevalent amongst the elderly. It is not clear whether this is because they do not understand their risks or because the consequences of victimization may generally be more severe for them. They are more likely to be injured, upset or seriously inconvenienced by crime than younger people (Clarke *et al.*, 1985). Whatever the reasons it is often stressed that, particularly for older people, the fear of crime is often more of a problem than crime itself. This fear can lead to self imposed 'house arrest' which is ironic as the evidence from recent research illustrates the vulnerability of elderly people in their own homes (Jones, 1987).

The research by Clarke identified three social determinants of fear of crime amongst elderly people. These were their percep-

Most crime involves property offences.

tions of the crime rate, their degree of social isolation and the nature of their immediate environment. Jones adds a fourth, arguing that personal self-image is also an important factor affecting the fear of crime since it is a common belief that elderly people, being more vulnerable through both physical weakness and social isolation, make ideal victims. In addition, the majority of elderly people are women, therefore not just age but gender stereotypes contribute to this weak picture since women have had these feelings all their lives.

In such a vulnerable situation fear may well be an appropriate response and it is difficult to know how to lower this. Jones'

Much crime is carried out by young people.

research indicated that when asked about the possible options for increasing the security of their environment most elderly people were in favour of community policing, that is, ensuring a visible police presence. Underwood (1984) suggested that a high police presence is unlikely to be effective as the young may view it as a challenge and it may even act as an encouragement to increase vandalism. Designing the built environment in order to minimalize the risk of crime is another option.

Although fear often reflects vulnerability to crime, fear of assault and burglary have become a serious problem even in some rural areas and small towns where levels of crime are low.

Such anxiety may be linked to reports of high urban crime rates that are thought to apply locally and to a disproportionate emphasis on violent and sexual offences and sensationalized reports of crime in local newspapers. The amount of crime that takes place should not be exaggerated, nor should the impact of crime on those most likely to be victims be understated. Experience or fear of crime is an everyday problem for many people. It needs to be dealt with by mobilizing the resources of local authorities, the community itself and the police.

1.3 THE EFFECT OF DESIGN ON CRIME

It has been argued that there are three basic elements necessary for a person to commit a crime: ability, opportunity and motive. The provision of building security through design attempts is to eliminate or reduce the intruder's ability and opportunity to commit a crime. This in turn should also reduce their motivation.

Bennett and Wright (1984) explored some of the assumptions underlying situational crime prevention and deterrence theory by obtaining the views of the offenders themselves. Their study of burglars' methods was based on information from burglars who had been caught. Although the validity of such responses is questionable, since these are failed burglars and successful ones might have different methods, their findings concurred with those of Jackson and Winchester (1982) from their study of both victims and non-victims of burglary in Kent.

Bennett and Wright found no clear connection between the physical environment and rates of burglary. However, they did identify surveillability and occupancy as the most important factors influencing burglars' choice of targets; this concurs with Jackson and Winchester's findings. Factors influencing the surveillability of the target included cover, presence and proximity of neighbours, whether the building was overlooked and if rear access existed. Risk cues relating to occupany included whether there was a car in the drive, a light on, or such evidence of occupancy as signs of a dog or a burglar alarm. Ease of access was affected by locks and the design of potential entry points.

The study found that most houses became the target for burglary for reasons independent of their degree of security. Targets were chosen partly because of the potential reward they may offer and because they were not occupied, but mostly because they could be easily approached without the burglar being seen. The importance of this concept of designing to deter and of natural surveillance is considered in greater detail in later chapters.

1.4 CRIME DISPLACEMENT

Bennett and Wright (1984) also indicated that casual burglars who seek targets are flexible and more likely to be displaced (i.e. will move onto another dwelling if prevented from entering the intended target), than offenders who planned one particular crime. The factors which were identified as exerting the greatest influence on displacement did not relate to 'reward' or 'ease of entry', but to 'risk of getting caught'. The most important risk factors were identified as surveillability and occupany. Bennett and Wright note that these results were not new (this information had been previously available): they stress that the only surprise is that it has not been exploited in crime prevention programmes.

The danger of crime displacement is sometimes given as justification for not tackling the security problem of an estate. However, research by Allatt (1984) indicates that displacement need not necessarily be as great a problem as originally envisaged. Allatt used police statistics and a two stage tenant survey to consider the effect of target hardening techniques on the improvement of residential security in an entire 'difficult to let' estate. Both the effect upon the high burglary rate in the estate itself and the displacement of burglary to two adjacent neighbourhoods or into other property crimes on the estate were considered. In contrast with a control estate, where burglary rose, Allatt's research indicated that burglary steadied for approximately one year and attempted burglary declined. Displacement effects were largely confined to the estate and overall crime was probably reduced.

1.5 TRADITIONAL APPROACHES TO CRIME PREVENTION

Until recently it was generally felt that responsibility for crime prevention lay with the police and individual householders. They alone, however, cannot solve the crime problem and deploying more police officers may have little or no effect on crime levels. Much police time is taken up in responding to crime after it has taken place, and the police do not have the resources or authority to intervene in many of the circumstances which lead to crime being committed. Individual householders, particularly the most vulnerable, may not be able to meet the full costs of securing their homes. In any case, for many areas, their efforts to protect themselves and their homes are likely to be successful only when they are part of a broader strategy aimed at reducing crime throughout a neighbourhood. In addition, crime is rarely the only or most serious problem in high crime areas, especially in areas of public sector housing. Estates with crime problems are also likely to be places where there has been little or no planned maintenance or investment, where housing services are poor, where there is high unemployment, or where there are few if any facilities for children and young people.

The traditional approaches to crime prevention also do little to address the causes of crime. They assume that a high level of crime is inevitable and that the public must defend itself against it. Campaigning too vigorously about crime may make elderly people and those who live alone fearful and anxious. Over-vigilant Neighbourhood Watch schemes could create an atmosphere of suspicion and conflict. A purely security based approach to crime prevention will also have no impact on domestic violence against women and children.

People who promote reactive, defensive approaches to crime may overlook the fact that a good deal of crime is committed by the young people of a neighbourhood, sometimes their own children and those of their neighbours. Young people may drift into crime through boredom or limited access to work or leisure opportunities. Much preventive effort could be usefully targeted towards them and it is important to bear in mind the very local nature of much crime. Designs which discourage outsiders from

Traditional approaches to crime prevention.

entering the neighbourhood may be counter-productive as they stem the healthy flow of passers-by and leave the field open to local miscreants.

Although buildings and their surroundings need to be designed with security in mind, over-reliance on defensive measures can create other problems. A 'fortress mentality' can develop where people lock themselves up in an atmosphere of isolation and mutual suspicion. Everyone's mobility and freedom is also potentially hampered if they have to cope with extra keys, entryphones, closed circuit television surveillance, burglar alarm over-rides, guard dogs and falsely triggered alarms on shops and houses. It is also possible that determined offenders may resort to greater force to achieve their ends and blatantly defensive hardware may even be seen as a challenge to the aspiring delinquent. There may also be a conflict between the interests of fire safety and the prevention of unlawful access.

1.6 DESIGN AND CRIME PREVENTION: A BROADER APPROACH

A broader approach to crime prevention is therefore necessary. This must focus on the role of local authorities and other public organizations as well as the police. It must address the particular needs of groups most vulnerable to crime. Such an approach should consider the relationship between levels of crime and the facilities, services and opportunities of particular neighbourhoods. It should attempt to divert young people from offending in the first place and encourage young offenders not to offend again. The term 'community safety' is used to reflect this broader approach. It is best achieved when a crime prevention strategy is part of a general programme of estate or neighbourhood regeneration.

It is important to recognize that although design measures can play a significant role in crime reduction, in most cases they need to be part of a larger package of safety improvements. Experience has shown that this package must also include management issues, facilities available in a neighbourhood (particularly those for young people) and the policing of residential areas. As this book concentrates on the role of the designer and the part they can play in the improvement of residential security, most emphasis will be placed on the design measures. The importance of the other issues, however, should not be understated.

This broader approach crosses many boundaries of concern and responsibility, so it is essential to enlist the involvement and support of all service delivery agencies in the area as well as local residents. Experience has shown that resident involvement and inter-agency co-operation are key factors in determining the lasting success of any community safety improvements.

This book considers the actions that architects, planners and housing managers can take to improve crime prevention through better design as part of this broader approach. It considers both the problems of new build housing for the private sector, and the difficult decisons which must be taken on the improvement of existing public sector estates.

The next chapter looks at various theories of security and in Chapter 3 a series of principles for designing to deter are extracted from these theories. Chapter 4 is concerned with the importance of assessment and resident pariticipation in decisions on the upgrade of existing estates. Chapters 5, 6 and 7 contain detailed guidance on the various aspects of design relevant to architects, planners and specifiers. Chapter 8 looks briefly at security during the construction process.

REFERENCES

Allat, P. (1984) Residential security: containment and displacement of burglary, *Howard Journal of Penology and Criminology*, **23** (2), 99–116.

Bennett, T. and Wright, R. (1984) *Burglars on Burglary, Prevention and the Offender*, Gower.

Clarke, R. *et al.*, (1985) Elderly victims of crime and exposure to risk, *Howard Journal of Criminal Justice*, **24** (1), 1–9.

Jackson, H. and Winchester, S. W. C. (1982) Which Houses are Burgled and Why?, in *Home Office Research Bulletin No 13*, (eds R. Walmsley, and L. Smith), Home Office Research and Planning Unit, London.

Jones, G. M. (1987) Elderly people and domestic crime: reflections on ageism, sexism and victimology, *British Journal of Criminology*, **27** (2), 191–201.

Middlesex Polytechnic (1990) *The Second Islington Crime Survey*, Centre for Criminology, Middlesex Polytechnic.

Rogers, M. R. *et al.*, (1989) *Quality of Life in Britain's Intermediate Cities*, University of Glasgow, Glasgow.

Scottish Office (1989) *Criminal Statistics, Scotland*, HMSO, Edinburgh.

Underwood, G. (1984) *The Security of Buildings*, Architectural Press Ltd, London.

FURTHER READING

Home Office *Criminal Statistics, England and Wales*, HMSO, London.

Mayhew, P. Elliott, D. and Dowds, L. (1989) *The 1988 British Crime Survey*, Home Office Research Study 111, HMSO, London.

Scottish Office (1988) *The British Crime Survey Scotland*, Scottish Office Central Research Unit, HMSO, London.

2 Theories of security design

This chapter considers a number of approaches to the analysis of security risks and the principle theories of security design. Although categorization of the various theories may differ, the basic concepts and ideas reoccur. Whilst most of the research and discussion focuses on the problems associated with high density public sector housing, the concepts considered are also applicable to lower density private housing.

Rand (1979) outlined four theories of crime prevention through environmental design: social control; enclose/access control; criminal justice; and defensible space. These are all based on the premise that multiple housing has inevitable side effects which are sometimes undesirable and that it is possible to develop guidelines to avoid these since crimes amongst strangers are, in part, a simple by-product of the numbers of unacquainted people who come in close physical contact.

Gardiner (1978) noted that designing for the defence of one's home is not a new concept, but age old. However, instead of defending against a recognized external enemy the enemy is now sometimes within the community. Gardiner outlines three conceptual models for the design of a safe environment: the urban village; the urban fortress; and defensible space. These categories roughly correspond with those proposed by Rand, with urban village equating with 'social control', and urban fortress combining both 'enclose/access control' and 'criminal justice'. Following Rands' classification these theories of crime prevention through environmental design will now be briefly considered in turn.

2.1 SOCIAL CONTROL

Based on the work of Jane Jacobs (1961) this approach suggests that streets are populated by strangers and that natural or passive surveillance (unconscious social control) will result from diversity of use. Business establishments provide people with a proprietary interest in the street directly in front of them, and shops give people a reason for using the streets. Jacob's view of the role of commercial facilities reversed the notion that these intensely public areas attracted crime.

2.2 ENCLOSE/ACCESS CONTROL

This is the traditional target hardening approach to security design. The theory is that if good security is provided at the perimeter of a community or multi-occupancy dwelling, the potential for live social interaction with the community increases and thus the likelihood of a stranger gaining access and committing a crime dimishes. The environment can be designed to discourage, even prevent, criminal access (e.g. airports are designed with security checks in order to prevent weapons being taken on board). Unfortunately even elaborate measures are not always certain to succeed. In the domestic environment smaller scale measures are suggested which range from residential door intercoms to complex alarm systems. However, in order for these to work, the community around which these security measures are implemented needs to be homogeneous. In addition the formation of such enclaves can, as previously noted, create problems by eliciting a more violent response from the external intruder or by the displacement of crime to the surrounding areas.

2.3 CRIMINAL JUSTICE

This approach focuses on the presence of a security force as a primary deterrent to crime. This may mean crime prevention through the presence of a high police profile or, as in parts of

Northern Ireland, the use of a military presence. The design of housing is focused on the provision of through roads giving optimum access for security patrols. Streets are laid out on a grid in order to provide clear unambiguous access allowing the opportunity for patrol cars to pass through all areas. Culs-de-sac are not used since these are viewed as dead ends and, in some cases, potential traps. Stollard (1984) gives an interesting example of one Catholic housing estate in Belfast where the Protestant rubbish collectors refused to make their rounds in the culs-de-sac for this very reason.

2.4 DEFENSIBLE SPACE

This approach suggests that crime is less likely when potential anti-social acts are framed in a physical space that is under surveillance. The effect of surveillance as a mechanism of social control increases when observers know each other or when they are linked by some common territorial marker. This theory goes on to suggest that potential criminals are more reluctant to commit crimes in the areas which are perceived to be under the technical influences of a surrounding community. This implicity suggests that a large number of crimes are spontaneous, occurring in response to opportunities which present themselves in anonymous settings.

Oscar Newman (1972) used the term 'defensible space' to describe the residential environment designed in such a way as to allow households to supervise, and to be seen to be responsible for, the areas in which they live. Newman proposed four constituents of good design to encourage the social control networks which he claims have been eroded by urbanization, the pressure of population, and new building techniques. These four measures were:

1. territoriality – the subdivision of buildings and grounds into zones of influence to discourage outsiders from entering and encourage residents to defend their areas;
2. surveillance – the design of buildings to allow easy observation of the related territory;

3. image – the design of public housing to avoid stigma;
4. environment – the juxtaposing of public housing projects with safe zones in adjacent areas.

Within this framework Newman considered how projects should be designed to reduce the risk of crime, with the emphasis being placed on the first two measures.

Newman's work has been widely criticized on two main counts. Firstly, because of the concentration on architectural determinism with too little attention paid to factors other than design. Secondly, on the methodological inadequacies of his research. Wilson (1978) conducted a comprehensive 'test' of Newman's ideas and found no direct relationship between design features and vandalism. She identified child density as the most crucial factor determining levels of reported vandalism.

As in 'enclose/access control' approaches, defensible space theory suggests that the creation of identifiable neighbourhoods through the use of definite boundaries allows residents to feel more of a sense of ownership over the space, this is based on the assumed idea of territoriality (i.e. individual and collective code response to environment). This will be considered in greater detail in the section on neighbourhoods (section 3.2). The security achieved by defensible space principles is symbolic. By creating multiple opportunities for surveillance and for the development of patterns of mutual accountability, the defensibly designed environment discourages crime by making people feel that they are known to others and will be held responsible to account for their behaviour.

Although these theories are presented as four different approaches, they are not mutually exclusive; in fact a comprehensive approach incorporating a mix is normally attempted.

2.5 THE CURRENT DEBATE

From his architectural deterministic approach to the built environment, Newman's later work expanded to acknowledge the fact that social, management and ownership variables need to be controlled in studying the effect of design. Newman suggested that safe housing areas are those where there is not only defensible space, but also good housing management in which tenants participate and residents are organized into homogeneous groups (e.g. by age and/or lifestyle). He referred to these groupings as 'communities of interest', though they could be considered as 'ghettos'.

Rand notes, unlike some other protagonists, that it is not housing itself which produces the negative side effects but the principles of social order that the housing design reflects. When mounting a strategy for attacking crime in the streets it is not possible to approach every aspect at once. Beginning with the housing design and layout will eventually have an effect on all other spheres.

Following on from the ideas of Newman, Poyner (1982) derived design implications which he summarized in the form of patterns. These patterns aim to reduce the opportunity for crime by removing targets, changing accessibility and increasing the natural surveillance qualities of both design and layout. Poyner also advocated the idea of 'communities of interest' stating that some form of common management or shared legal responsibility for the street should be included in a neighbourhood. He suggests that the creation of homogeneous neighbourhoods should be encouraged by the separation of housing from commercial uses and of wealthy from poorer housing.

Coleman (1985) carried out research for the Home Office on the relationship between the incidence of crime and the design of the built environment. Like Newman and Poyner, she also adopts a deterministic approach, suggesting that certain design features encourage high levels of crime and social breakdown. She identified 28 specific design variables (16 for flats, 12 for houses) which she associates with progressive environmental degradation, family breakdown, health problems and crime. She argues that as each variable becomes more intense, and as more of these variables occur in combination, so the environment deteriorates.

Like Newman before her, Coleman has been widely criticized for a lack of coherent methodology. However, like Newman, Coleman proposed neat and precise design criteria as solutions to the urban problem thus gaining a strong following amongst

those requiring simplistic solutions. Coleman argues ve-
hemently that by transforming the problem designs of modern
movement architecture into something resembling the 'naturally
evolved norm' of the inter-war period, the significant social
mores will begin to echo those of 'that low crime period'. This
indicates an apparent belief, a Utopian idealism, in a previous
golden age of low crime; the validity of which is questionable.
Hillier (1986) for example, suggests that such an idealistic view
of the past, which he claims is often misinterpreted, has helped
to create the urban problems currently experienced, whilst
Shapland (1988) notes that discussion about informal social
control is ridden with stereotypes concerning a mythical golden
age when communities were close and sorted their own problems out, aided by the friendly local bobby. The fact that this
closeness was in itself restricting is conveniently overlooked.

2.6 PRINCIPLES NOT DESIGN GUIDES

Whilst suspicious of simplistic, deterministic arguments, Jenks
(1988) acknowledged that designers wanted simple and easy
certainties which are readily absorbed, digested and incorporated into the design. Unfortunately, ideas which are easily
latched onto appeal, even when there is no sound basis for them.
The work of both Newman and Coleman has been strongly
criticized on methodological grounds (e.g. Adams, 1973), but
because their research offers concepts which can be easily
implemented they have been widely followed.

Bearing these limitations in mind this book attempts in the
following chapters both the impossible and the inappropriate,
that is to derive such simple certainties from the existing
literature and practice. Whilst general agreement exists concerning the particular principles which are important in maxi-
mizing the security of dwellings, the proposed methods or design
options for achieving these stated objectives vary. The next
chapter considers a series of key principles relevant to all
architects, planners and housing managers and the remaining
chapters look at the application of these principles in newbuild
and existing housing.

REFERENCES

Adams, J. (1973) *DRS Journal: Design research and methods*, **7** (3), 266–7.

Coleman, A. (1985) *Utopia on Trial*, Hilary Shipman, London.

Gardiner, R. A. (1978) *Design for Safe Neighbourhoods: The environment planning and design process*, A United States Government Information Product.

Hillier, B. (1986) City of Alice's Dreams, *Architects' Journal*, **184** (28), 39–41.

Jacobs, J. (1961) *The Death and Life of Great American Cities*, Jonathan Cape, London. (Also published by Penguin Books Ltd, 1965.)

Jenks, M. (1988) Housing problems and the dangers of certainty, design process and scientific inquiry, in *Rehumanising Housing* (eds Teymeur, Markus and Woolley), Butterworth.

Newman, O. (1972) *Defensible Space: People and design in the violent city*, Macmillan, New York.

Poyner, B. (1982) *Crime Prevention through Environmental Design and Management: An overview*, Home Office Research and Planning Unit (Research bulletin No 131) HMSO, London, 2–5.

Rand, G. (1979) Multiple housing security through environmental design, in *Handbook of Building Security, Planning and Design* (ed. P. S. Hopf) McGraw Hill.

Shapland, J. (1988) Policing with the Public, in *Communities and Crime Reduction*, Home Office Research and Planning Unit, HMSO, London, 116–25.

Stollard, P. J. (1984) The Architecture of No-Mans Land, *Architects' Journal*, **180** (31), 24–41.

Wilson, S. (1978) Vandalism and 'defensible space' on London Housing Estates, in *Tackling Vandalism*, Home Office Research Study No 47.

3

Six principles

Having recognized that dissension exists over the appropriate design options to employ in order to deter crime, it should be noted that there is some common agreement over general principles. Along the continuum of opinion, which ranges from environmental determinists, to those who are sceptical of the influence the built environment exerts over crime, it is agreed that all design and layout solutions must be site specific if they are to achieve any degree of success. There is also agreement on a series of essentials in designing to deter: this chapter will consider six of these key principles for architects, designers, planners and housing managers.

3.1 SURVEILLANCE

The first such principle concerns natural or passive surveillance of both dwellings and the surrounding public spaces. This is widely considered to be the most basic and essential element of deterring crime by making intruders feel conspicuous. Natural surveillance can be defined as the impression that residents are keeping, or are able to keep, an eye on their neighbour's and their own property. This idea of surveillance extends beyond the individual's or neighbour's property to public or communal spaces such as childrens' play areas, car parking spaces, shops and other community facilities, footpaths and access points. Opportunist crime is likely to be reduced if the potential offender feels there is, or may be, someone watching.

Architects and planners must consider the options available to maximize the residents opportunities to keep an eye on their neighbourhood: these range from the careful assignment of space to specific houses or particular blocks, to the siting of car

Surveillance.

parking and play areas where they can be overlooked by a number of dwellings. Dwelling orientation is particularly significant in determining the amount of natural surveillance provided in an estate and this is also considered in the later section on neighbourhoods (section 3.2).

It is interesting to note that recent work by Shapland (1988) found that the public have a largely incorrect perception of burglars, indicating that the things people watch for and report may not necessarily be aiding security. This finding does not detract from the need to design for the possibility of natural surveillance since, as noted earlier, Bennett and Wright (1984) found that, whether used or not, natural surveillance was an important factor in deterring casual burglars. Whilst the Department of Environment guidance (Bennett *et al.*, 1984) stresses that it does not matter whether surveillance takes place, the important thing is to create an environment which makes an intruder feel conspicuous. However, the discrepancy high-lighted by Shapland does emphasize the need for education. Information is not only required on who commits crimes, but also how often and where these crimes occur since considerable problems are associated with the discrepancies which exist between actual crime rates and the fear of crime.

Shapland and Vagg (1987, 1988), like Jacobs (1961), found that local shops, in particular shops with something outside on the pavement (either advertising or goods) acted as important focal points for the discussion and dissemination of information concerning the neighbourhood. Such informal policing is an essential element of any successful crime prevention scheme, for example Neighbourhood Watch. It seems a waste to design to enable people to supervise their neighbourhood if they do nothing with the information they are given. Both education, so that people recognize what they see and are not blinded by outdated prejudices, and informal gathering points for the dissemination of information could be encouraged, supporting the idea of the collaborative approach to security which is discussed later in this chapter.

3.2 NEIGHBOURHOODS

Linked with the principle of surveillance is that of neighbour-hoods. The majority of researchers and practitioners favour the concept of territoriality, that is, the idea that people identify with, watch over and protect their own particular neighbour-hood. It is argued that designing layouts which foster a sense of neighbourliness or community will contribute towards making intruders feel conspicuous, since residents will be more able to identify who does or does not belong.

Gardiner (1978) discusses 'environmental security' which he defines as an urban planning design process which integrates crime prevention with neighbourhood design and urban de-velopment. This is not only concerned with design details, but also education in order to reduce the fear of crime. He notes that the basic problem in dealing with the 'neighbourhood unit' is the fact that there is no accepted dimension or shape, no ubiquitous formula or model by which to define the neighbourhood. The boundaries of the local neighbourhood will vary according to the view of the person who defines it. For example, someone who spends most if not all of their day in the home will probably have a rather different definition of neighbourhood compared with someone who travels to work in the town centre. Most research focuses on inner city, high density estates and indicates that informal social control is not possible today because of the lack of cohesion in the modern neighbourhood. However, Shapland's research, which was based in rural areas, also stressed the importance of informal social control.

Whilst noting the problems in defining local neighbourhoods Gardiner identifies certain common physical and social characteristics which contribute to a successful neighbourhood. He suggests that a successful neighbourhood is a place where an individual has certain inherent personal and property rights, including control over their home, business and immediate surroundings, a place which gives a sense of security which is intrinsically a part of the notion of home as a safe place, and a place which generates a confidence to invest. It possesses particular physical boundaries and focal points which, while perhaps not clearly readable to the non-resident, provide a sense of place or personal identity for the resident. It has certain essential public and private support services (e.g. roads, schools, parks, shops) within which unstated standards of behaviour based upon community interests, concerns and group values are expected.

Poyner (1983), like Newman (1980), argued for 'communities of interest'; that is, the creation of homogeneous neighbourhoods by combining residents with similar ages, life styles and aspirations. Whilst the creation of such 'ghettos' is not generally advocated, the idea of less homogeneous yet readily identifiable neighbourhoods is more widely supported.

Having considered the concept of neighbourhood in relation to the design principle of territoriality, it is important to note that despite its widespread influence on and inclusion in theories of environmental security design it is not a universally held truth. Hillier (1988) argues convincingly against the concept of neighbourhood. He challenges the way in which such concepts have been borrowed from the natural sciences and refers to territoriality as 'an ignorant view of human nature which has largely been discredited by anthropological research'.

Hillier notes that a predominant theme in most recent housing (from the philanthropic estates of the nineteenth century through to those more recently proposed by the Greater London Council) is the idea of the social value of small, self-identifying communities. This concept has influenced the provision of a hierarchical and disjointed urban landscape. Hillier argues that the idea of such localized enclosures where a well defined space is uniquely associated with the buildings that open on to it is not the answer to the urban problem, but rather the problem itself. He states that the indiscriminate use of enclosures is responsible for the creation of fragmentary and under used spaces where little happens: the 'urban desert' effect. Hillier advocates an alternative to inward facing, self absorbed neighbourhood communities, stating that since research indicates that a higher proportion of burglaries occur in segregated areas, open outward facing layouts with integration given priority over exclusion and group territory are a more appropriate design solution.

3.3 PUBLIC AND PRIVATE SPACES

The third key principle is closely related to the concept of neighbourhood and concerns the importance of distinguishing between public and private space. It has already been noted that Newman's initial approach (1972) to security design was based on a complex hierarchy of public, semi-public, semi-private and private space. Other approaches to security design advocate alternative ways of organizing space. Whatever the approach adopted towards dwelling grouping and orientation, a general consensus exists over the importance of strict differentiation between public and private space.

Part of Hillier's argument on neighbourhood concerns the tendency in modern design layouts to make public space increasingly more private. Instead of creating neighbourliness as intended, such designs ensure that this privatized public space is in fact an 'urban desert', an area no one uses and no one cares about, and this leads to a higher incidence of crime. Hillier suggests that old, 'successful' towns are comprised of an interconnected network of public spaces. Visual links give both a sense of scale and help to differentiate between the public and the private areas. These visual links enable people to relate each particular space to the whole town. He belives that the concept of very private dormitory estates located on the periphery of towns has extended the idea of privacy too far creating 'urban deserts' and that such unused private spaces should be made public again.

Alternatively the use of layouts where dwellings are designed in small clusters have been widely recommended in design guides, for example Essex (Essex County Council, 1973). These propose small identifiable neighbourhood units with limited public access. The main aim being to create an environment which encourages neighbourliness and, through this, natural surveillance and self-policing, so making intruders conspicuous and, hopefully, discouraging crime.

3.4 POTENTIAL HIDING PLACES

The fourth principle is less controversial and concerns the importance of eliminating potential hiding places: places where intruders might lurk undetected and commit acts of violence unobserved should be avoided.

3.5 COMPREHENSIVE APPROACHES

The fifth widely accepted principle involves the adoption of a comprehensive approach. Design and layout should be considered in conjunction with other security strategies, such as target hardening measures and informal policing by the community. These different strategies need to be incorporated into a comprehensive package. Underwood (1984), considering vandalism, suggested an approach incorporating elements of defensible space, fortressing and management. The NHBC (1986)

Potential hiding places.

advocates that a similar balance should be maintained in the precautions taken. They suggest that the precautions to take are, in order of priority:

1. more secure site layout;
2. security of private areas including safer car parking;
3. making entry into dwellings more difficult.

Their guidelines recognize that on some schemes, due to the limits of site layout and the types of dwellings being built to provide the best natural surveillance or defences, it may be necessary to compensate for security deficiencies by increasing the resistance of likely points of entry. It is suggested that if it is not possible to provide the best natural surveillance or defences it will be necessary to compensate by increasing the resistance of likely points of entry. Such target hardening is not simply concerned with the addition of locks and bolts, it also requires a consideration of the details of the design.

The NHBC also argues that the adoption of the principles of providing a well-lit, small, self-policing, community where intruders will be easily observed produces a well liked attractive layout which many builders are already adopting to meet the wishes of their customers. Many of the recommended measures can be incorporated at the design state without incurring extra costs (e.g. the way dwellings are linked together to form their own secure boundary can also be done in such a way as to minimize the cost of gates and fencing).

3.6 COLLABORATIVE APPROACHES

The sixth and final principle for architects and planners to consider is concerned primarily with large public sector estates. Here collaboration by all relevant bodies is crucial. This collaboration has two aspects, first the importance of the daily management of the completed estate and secondly, the inclusion of management in the design process.

Power, who has spearheaded the department of the Environment's Priority Estates Programme (PEP), rejects the view that design alone can explain the problems in public rented housing, arguing that rented housing requires good landlords, regardless of design (Power, 1987). The PEP works with the local authority to improve the run-down housing estates which have become unpopular and difficult to manage. The Estate Action team (formerly the Urban Housing Renewal Unit) provides both information and training, depending on the local authorities requirements, in order to assist it in implementing the PEP programme, which is based on the idea of local, decentralized estate based housing management. A local, full-time housing management office is set up in each estate with devolved responsibility/authority and budget to enable all the estate management, including allocations, rent collection and repairs and maintenance to be locally controlled. Co-ordination with other council services is encouraged in order to achieve improvments across the board. In addition to the PEP improvement approach, the remit of the Estate Action team is to develop alternative initiatives including transfers of ownership and/or management to tenants trust or co-operatives and the sale of both tenanted and empty properties for refurbishment for sale and for rent.

It is important, obviously, to include all the available information when deciding on the design options for a particular site. The Safe Neighbourhoods Unit (SNU) urges that all interested parties, tenants and the wide range of agencies which work in the field including social services, probation and police (either architecture liaison, community or crime prevention officers), are involved in each project. The co-ordination of different agencies not only enables all the available information to be utilized, but allows different sources of finance to be tapped.

Estate based, tenant orientated approaches to housing security which place considerable emphasis on management techniques are perhaps more appropriate for existing public housing estates, though some basic principles, such as the inclusion of a high level of estate based management and caretaking, could be incorporated into new build schemes in the private sector.

Some researchers, for example Lawrence (1987) and Shapland (1988), call for the breakdown of barriers, both professional and academic, which exist between diverse groups of people who study the residential environment as well as between those who design and manage them. Lawrence suggests that one way in which to bridge the chasm between architects and lay people is by the formation of housing co-ops. However, this does not necessarily follow: sometimes the process only serves to highlight the differences between the two groups and co-ops are not necessarily the most appropriate form of housing for everyone. Poyner (1983) suggests that some form of common management or shared legal responsibility for the street would encourage the neighbourhood ethos and, following defensible space strategies, would help to reduce the risk of crime.

In addition Shapland notes the importance of co-ordination between the Home Office, the Department of the Environment and other organizations engaged in research in this field. She suggests that one way in which this might be achieved is through the inclusion of design orientated questions as standard in any police crime statistical survey. For example, these questions could be introduced into the current national revision of the police coding frame, providing a standard source for relevant design statistics. This would enable designers to readily acquire appropriate design information. At present only details concerning the offender are recorded such as age, race and gender; in future it should be possible to include information about the offence itself, for example where crimes occur, what types of dwelling are attacked, or how entry was made.

This sixth principle of ensuring a collaborative approach extends the responsibility for security to people other than the architects and planners. However their role remains significant, because of the advantages of incorporating preventative measures in future housing over rectifying designed mistakes with short-term policing or mopping-up solutions.

REFERENCES

Bennett, G., Noble, J. and Jenks, M. (1984) *More than Just a Road*, Information Directorate, DoE, HMSO, London.

Bennett, T. and Wright, R. (1984) *Burglars on Burglary, Prevention and the Offender*, Gower.

Essex County Council (1973) *Essex Design Guide for Residential Areas*, Anchor Press Ltd.

Gardiner, R. A. (1978) *Design for Safe Neighbourhoods: The environment planning and design process*, A United States Government Information Product.

Hillier, B. (1988) Against Enclosure, in *Rehumanising Housing* (eds Treymeur, Markus and Woolley), Butterworth,

Jacobs, J. (1961) *The Death and Life of Great American Cities*, Jonathan Cape, London. (Also published by Penguin Books Ltd, 1965.)

Lawrence, R. J. (1987) *Housing, Dwellings and Homes: Design theory, research and practice*, John Wiley and Sons, New York.

National House-building Council (NHBC) (1986) *Guidance on how the Security of New Homes can be Improved*, NHBC,

Newman, O. (1972) *Defensible Space: People and design in the violent city*, Macmillan, New York.

Newman, O. (1980) *Community of Interest*, Anchor Press/Double Day, New York.

Power, A. (1987) *Property Before People: The management of twentieth century council housing*, Allen and Unwin,

Poyner, B. (1983) *Design Against Crime: Beyond defensible space*, Butterworths,

Shapland, J. (1988) Policing with the Public, in *Communities and Crime Reduction*, Home Office Research and Planning Unit, HMSO, London, 116–25.

Shapland, J. and Vagg, J. (1987) Using the Police, *British Journal of Criminology*, **27** (1), 54–63.

Shapland, J. and Vagg, J. (1988) *Policing by the Public*, Routledge, London.

Underwood, G. (1984) *The Security of Buildings*, Architectural Press Ltd, London.

4

Assessment process – existing estates

There are no standard solutions which can be used in the re-designing of existing estates in order to reduce crime. Each estate or neighbourhood has to be carefully analysed and assessed to establish its strengths and weaknesses. The whole spectrum of services and facilities impinging on the area may have to be studied: design; layout; physical security; management; repairs and maintenance; lettings policy; policing; tenant/resident mix; child density; play and youth facilities; lighting; transport arrangements; social facilities. Security and safety matters cannot be considered in isolation and it is necessary to draw up a full picture of the problems and needs of an area before embarking on an improvement programme.

4.1 PROJECT STEERING COMMITTEES

At the outset, it is important to have an effective project steering committee. Its structure will depend on local circumstance, but would usually include representatives from all key council departments, from local voluntary organizations, from the police, and from any residents' organizations. It is also important that the steering committee contains officers and/or members of the local authority with sufficient power and discretion to make decisions and act quickly. Where re-design and rehabilitation are likely to be major components of estate improvements, the project architect would normally be a member of this steering committee. In some circumstances, however, the steering committee may be the 'client' which commissions the architect, who would remain a professional contractor, rather than a group member. In many cases this committee would have to be specially formed for the purposes of the project. In some other cases it may be possible to use a committee or forum which is already in existence, for example, a neighbourhood committee or estate forum. Leadership is crucial and the committee needs to be chaired by a member or senior officer who has general support and the necessary authority to implement committee decisions.

In the case of public housing, it cannot be assumed that estates of a similar design type or size will share the same problems, or that a package of improvements that has worked in one area can be applied generally. Apart from the design, its size, location, range of household types, management and many other factors will influence the nature of proposed solutions. The purpose of assessment is to identify precisely what the problems are, how they interrelate and what combination of improvements (physical, managerial, community based) is required for each estate. It is best if this assessment is undertaken by a multi-disciplinary team of officers and professionals, working closely with the residents to ensure that no one perspective is allowed to dominate. An assessment of an estate by an architect, or a surveyor, or a housing manager, or a residents' leader on their own is likely to be limited and incomplete. However, working together, it is more likely that all the necessary elements of an improvement plan will be identified.

It is very much easier to secure a co-ordinated response to problems in areas of single tenure, such as local authority housing estates, than in those areas where there is a mixture of private rented, housing association, council and owner-occupied property. The difficulties of mounting initiatives in mixed tenure areas reflect the fact that their boundaries are less well defined than those of council estates and it is often difficult to decide on the size of the area to be covered. There is also likely to be a much wider range of concerns than in council estates, where attention is usually focused on council services, particularly repairs and management. In mixed tenure areas there are often a large number of interest or pressure groups representing a range of concerns, often competing with each other for limited resources. On council estates, residents' pressure group activities tend to be subsumed within one or two residents' organizations. It can also be difficult on mixed tenure estates to identify the local political and decision-making networks, while on council estates there is usually a well-understood system for trying to get things done (e.g. via the residents association).

It is therefore necessary, first of all, to obtain the agreement of a range of local organizations on where attention should be focused and what matters should be addressed. This may involve establishing new groups of individuals with shared interests, or setting up an action group comprising representatives from all local agencies and interest groups.

Having established a framework for consultation and decision making there are three main aspects of assessment: **consultation** with residents and local staff; **research** and collation of data on the estate or neighbourhood; **physical survey** of the condition of the estate or neighbourhood. Only when all the necessary information has been collected by assessment is it possible to begin the preparation of an estate plan containing proposals for improvement. Only once such an estate plan has been established can the difficult decisions be taken on which proposals should have priority.

4.2 CONSULTATION

Residents should have the opportunity to be involved throughout the whole process of improving the area or estate and there are many ways in which this can be done. In general, it is preferable for residents' representatives to have delegated authority to make decisions on a full range of issues, or at least to form the majority of any committee that has such authority.

It is much easier for residents to participate if there is an association in existence through which they can become involved. A system of block or street committees/representatives often works well. Where no association exists at the start of an improvement project, it may be necessary to set one up by

Consultation.

calling estate, street, or block meetings and inviting residents to form a group and become involved.

Consultation should take place with the residents in all blocks or streets, ensuring that there is proper representation according to gender, race and age. This can be done through small group meetings with representative groups of residents and local agencies. Alternatively there may be consultations with specific groups in the community such as young people, elderly people, single parents, shift workers and disabled people.

The techniques for consultation are many. They include questionnaires (household or self-completion surveys), or exhibitions of proposed options leading to discussions. Nominal group techniques can be used, where controlled groups of up to ten people brainstorm, feedback and ballot, to produce a structured range of improvement priorities (Delbecq *et al.*, 1975). There could be manipulative display techniques, in which small groups of people can choose their priorities and plan improvements by card sorting and re-arranging models of room, building and estate layouts (Lunzer and Gibson, 1979).

There may not be a suitable forum at which the concerns and priorities of established local groups and agencies can be promptly articulated; a questionnaire survey may be necessary to identify these concerns and priorities. An action group made up of these local groups and agencies could be established, which would respond positively to the survey and agree which organization should take the lead for each problem area identified. Such an investigation may identify a number of proposals which do not need further consultation. For example, local community groups may agree to share in the use and management of a re-designed community facility. Other proposals will need further assessment, through the processes of community consultation, data collection and surveys of the physical condition of the neighbourhood.

4.3 RESEARCH

Some research involving the collation of data on the estate/neighbourhood, its problems and its requirements will need to be undertaken. This could involve:

1. drawing up a demographic profile of the area or estate;
2. obtaining statistical information from the housing authority (repair backlogs, voids, level of demand, resident turnover, transfer applications, costs of vandalism, right to buy take-ups, downtimes of lifts and entry phones, cost of repairs to lifts and entry phones, level of rent arrears);
3. observing patterns of pedestrian and vehicular movement, involving measuring how levels vary at all times of the day, ideally in all seasons;
4. assessing levels of antisocial and criminal behaviour, which can be carried out by systematic observation, consultation with the police, social services departments and youth services, household questionnaire surveys and resident consultations;
5. obtaining information on the availability of key facilities and services, such as shops, schools, playgroups, youth clubs, public transport, health centres, residents' organizations and recreational opportunities;
6. housing management policy – lettings, child ratio, maintenance and repair programme, decentralization;

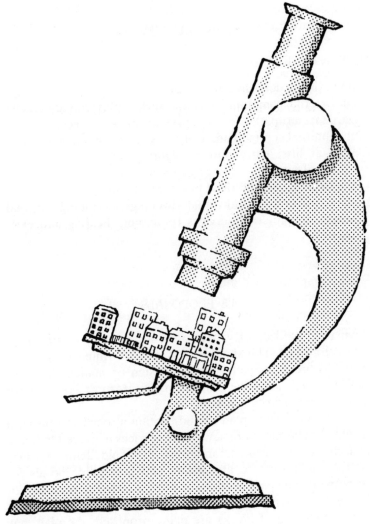

Research.

7. surveying effectiveness of existing crime prevention measures, crime surveys, etc, if any.

4.4 PHYSICAL SURVEYS

This may involve surveys of:

1. any existing defensive measures;
2. the external community facilities such as playgrounds, roads, gardens, footpaths, fencing, parking areas, garages;
3. the internal common areas of blocks and communal services such as lifts, entry phones, lighting, refuse disposal and means of escape;
4. the structure and fabric of blocks and houses;
5. the condition of individual dwellings, including internal spaces and internal services (plumbing, heating and electricity).

4.5 PROPOSALS

Having collected all relevant information the area or estate plan can be drawn up. This should attempt to determine whether the problems are principally physical/design or managerial, how they interrelate and which improvements are most likely to have an impact on security and safety.

The area or estate plan should contain a social and physical profile of the estate, a review of the services delivered to it and an account of its problems and needs. It should identify reasons for the decline of the area/estate and present proposals for reversing it. The plan needs to be presented to the residents for their endorsement at a series of meetings. When design changes and remodelling of blocks are being proposed, the plan may contain a number of options rather than firm recommendations. Exhibitions with drawings and models together with further block or street meetings will be necessary for officers and residents to discuss these options in detail and work towards preferred solutions. To avoid raising false expectations these should take place after the council and other local agencies have agreed to provide resources and to carry out the improvements.

4.6 PRIORITIES

There will rarely be sufficient resources to implement all the proposals and it will be necessary to determine which are the priorities. Often difficult decisions can be justified by reference to the findings from the research and consultation process. In other cases, there may be competing priorities between, for example, internal and external improvements, between the views of the residents and those of the professionals, or between the views of different groups of residents. Where there are no clear directions from the research/consultation process, resolution of such dilemmas will depend on the severity of particular problems and the strength of feeling about which improvements should receive priority. It is therefore essential that resident's representatives are involved at all stages of the discussions and that these are conducted in a forum considered to be fair and representative of all views. Draft plans and priorities must also be submitted to the body of residents for discussion and endorsement.

The particular needs of women should be recognized in the selection of priorities. Women are more often the victims of predatory crimes such as sexual assault and theft from the person. Fear of such crimes can be very high among women and many take what should be regarded as unacceptable levels of evasive action, such as avoiding going out alone or after dark. It is important for designers to promote a range of facilities and services to help prevent women becoming victims of crime, for example, by the creation of safe routes through estates and town centres with particular attention paid to lighting and surveillance.

People from ethnic minority groups are especially vulnerable to violent crime. They tend to be over-represented in disadvantaged areas which have higher levels of property crime and crime against the person than more prosperous neighbourhoods.

Racially motivated crime is a serious and growing problem in many areas. However, victims are often unwilling to report incidents and the police may be reluctant to treat incidents as 'crime'. The most persistent and debilitating forms of harassment take place on housing estates. Consulting communities, particularly black communities, about crime can be a difficult and sensitive matter. Many white people believe that black people are disproportionately responsible for certain types of crime, a view which stereotypes them and generates hostility. As a result, crime prevention initiatives mounted by local authorities or other agencies may be regarded suspiciously as attempts to further stigmatize black communities; this is particularly the case when the agencies concerned are largely white. If local authorities are to tackle crime in black communities they need to gain the confidence of black people by convincing them that they will also do something about discrimination and victimization.

Elderly people are often as concerned about 'incivilities' such as litter, dog nuisance, neighbour noise, car parking and broken pavements as they are about crime. Home alarm systems are good for summoning help as a result of any emergency, whether crime, illness or accident. Some local authorities make grants available to low-income, elderly owner-occupiers to enable them to purchase security equipment and have it installed. It is important that housing managers and landlords should remind elderly people at regular intervals to use security devices and check the identity of callers.

4.7 CASE STUDY OF THE ASSESSMENT PROCESS

In 1988 as a response to the problems of crime and the fear of crime associated with poor lighting, the London Borough of Brent commissioned the Safe Neighbourhoods Unit to carry out a study of public lighting provision on three priority estates: Stonebridge, Chalkhill and South Kilburn. The study was concerned with communal lighting within blocks of flats, lighting surrounding the blocks and lighting on routes into and around the estates. A Lighting and Safety Project Steering Committee which included officers from the Council's Joint Neighbourhood

Projects, Housing Department, Works Department, Central Race Unit, Womens Unit and Police Committee directed and monitored the study.

The assessment process consisted of a number of elements. Initially data was collected on the demography of the estates; police crime statistics were gathered; research was undertaken on the pattern of pedestrian and traffic circulation and on the nature of public transport services; and a review was undertaken of the local housing services, policing and community facilities.

Secondly, a programme of consultations was carried out with local residents and staff from the Council and other agencies. The purpose of the consultation was to identify the scale and location of problems associated with lighting and to draw up proposals for this, and other, improvements. Qualitative data was obtained through consultation meetings with small groups of residents on each estate and through meetings with residents associations, community groups, voluntary organizations, the police and Council officers. Quantitative data was obtained by means of a self-completion questionnaire administered to 400 households, with 202 completed questionnaires returned.

Thirdly, a lighting designer carried out a technical survey of the three estates, drawing up his recommendations to respond to residents' concerns and priorities. The recommendations included details of where lights should be positioned, the types of lamps to be used, the lux levels to be achieved and repair and maintenance procedures which should be introduced.

The final recommendations were prepared in consultation with the Project Steering Committee and residents associations, and also included proposals for associated improvements to block and dwelling security and estate policing. The study was funded by the Urban Programme.

REFERENCES

Delbecq *et al.* (1975) *Group Techniques for Programme Planning*, Illinois (out of print but synopsis available from SNU).

Lunzer, E. and Gibson, A. (1979) *Decision-making and the Language of Manipulative Display*, School of Education, University of Nottingham, Nottingham.

FURTHER READING

Department of the Environment, Estate Action (1989) *Handbook of Estate Improvement: Volume 1, Guidance on Option Appraisal*, HMSO, London.

Institute of Housing and RIBA (1988) *Tenant Participation in Housing Design*, RIBA Publications Limited, London.

Osborn, S. and Bright, J. (1989) *Crime Prevention and Community Safety: A practical guide for local authorities*, National Safe Neighbourhoods, London.

Safe Neighbourhoods Unit (1989) *Lighting Up Brent: Survey into lighting and safety on Chalk Hill, Stonebridge and South Kilburn Estates*,

5 Design process – site

During the design process the architects and planners must be aware of both the long-term and short-term security consequences of their decisions. In the short-term they should ensure that the upgrading process is as simple and painless as possible. The 'buildability' of the proposals is crucial: how easy it is to construct without causing further problems? These principles need to be applied to each aspect of the design.

In the long-term they need to consider how the improvements they make will be 'managed'. This will involve designing to reduce the amount of maintenance necessary and to make repair and replacement simple and inexpensive. They must be conscious of the future revenue consequences of their decisions as well as the short-term capital costs.

This chapter and the following two chapters consider a number of issues of design related both to new buildings and existing housing, where both long-term and short-term issues must be considered. This chapter considers issues related to the site. Chapter 6 considers the detail design process in the context of flats, and Chapter 7 examines the problems of individual houses.

5.1 PUBLIC OPEN SPACE

Experience has shown that communal space usually only works if it is managed by or on behalf of the residents who use it, but this does not mean that the provision of such should always be avoided. Communal space is sometimes appropriate, and there are many cases where it is not possible to convert it into private or public space, even if this were thought desirable (e.g. the communal areas within blocks). Any public space should come under natural surveillance from the surrounding dwellings.

Traditionally the provision of play areas has been associated with public housing, although as some private developers become involved in what was previously public property, or in the development of 'villages' within the green belt, interest may be generated. If sites are planned with culs-de-sac and through roads incorporating 'traffic calming' measures, children will be encouraged to play in the streets and appropriate measures should be taken to ensure that adequate provision is made so that they will not be encouraged to play around parked cars. Where play areas are provided they should be kept small and placed under natural surveillance, though not too close to residential dwellings.

5.2 FOOTPATHS

There should be a limited number of well-used, well-lit footpaths into and through an estate, ideally overlooked by a number of dwellings or building entrances. Passing vehicles can also provide casual surveillance of footpaths beside roads and reassurance to pedestrians, providing that some measures are taken to ensure that vehicular speed and volume is reduced. Where access routes do not generate much traffic it is even more important that they are overlooked by the frontages of dwellings.

In new developments, unnecessary footpaths, particularly those which do not follow vehicle routes and which might provide intruders with unobserved access and escape routes through and around estates, should be avoided. If the choice of layout makes separate footpaths necessary, they should be kept short, direct and well lit. Long, dark alleyways should be avoided at all costs. When providing access to the rear of terraced property, paths should not join to make a through route, though it is generally recommended to avoid rear access where possible.

Entrance features reinforce a sense of privacy.

A high proportion of vandalism can be attributed to people taking short cuts between lines of circulation. Sharp changes in direction should be avoided, and where unavoidable feeble items such as litter bins or low walls should not be used to change direction. Changes in materials, levels, or landscaping can be used to produce interesting and logical changes of movement; landscaping and planting associated with footpaths should reinforce security. As a general rule landscaping should not exceed one metre where abutting pavements, thus ensuring that it does not obstruct lighting or 'bush' out to form a hiding place.

The most extreme examples of uncontrolled pedestrian access are in estates where blocks of flats or maisonettes are freestanding in open space. Public access can then be restricted by enclosing the space around blocks with a communal garden or private gardens for ground floor dwellings. Where essential routes are neither well-used or overlooked, as is the case with the internal corridors of linear blocks, it may be necessary to restrict access to residents only.

It is not always easy to impose restrictions on the established routes of people within residential areas. Attempts are sometimes made to divert people away from familiar or convenient routes by the use of fences or other barriers. However these routes can be quickly re-established by damaging the barrier or by using gates provided for emergency access only. Proper consultation with residents and observations of pedestrian movements are essential if any re-organization of routes and footpaths is to achieve the intended objectives. It is important to note that 'desire lines' may only be established after a period of occupancy and flexibility should be incorporated into the design layout. In addition the shortest route may not necessarily be the desired route. In one estate in Southwark residents petitioned for a change in the footpath which led directly from their homes to local shops, because this was being used as a race track by local youths. Closure of this route and the provision of an alternative, which was less direct, proved to be both successful with residents and not as attractive to the racing fraternity.

The design, detailing and construction of any fence or barrier which closes off a short cut, or convenient but unauthorized route, must be carefully considered. Local authorities have usually found it cost effective to invest in high quality barriers, as even robust two metre high wooden perimeter fencing can start to deteriorate after four to five years. Any features made of wood are less resistant to the elements and need regular maintenance. They are also more vulnerable to attack by vandals: screws and nails can be pulled out and wood burns or breaks more easily than other materials.

5.3 CAR PARKING

Parking provision for residents should be located as close as possible to the owners dwelling, in order to ensure the casual surveillance of parked cars. If possible car parking should be located in individual garages within the curtilage of the dwelling, with the approach and entrance visible to occupants. The position of garages and car-ports should not obscure the general view.

Where there is no alternative to the provision of larger areas of communal off street parking they should be divided into small groups so that occupiers can become familiar with the cars and their owners, and thereby detect intruders. Unassigned parking spaces should be off the road in small, private, well-lit groups under natural surveillance and as close as possible to the dwellings. These should be blended in with the street rather than screened or obscured behind planting. Surrey police noted that theft of, or from, motor vehicles accounts for a quarter of all reported crime. They suggest that one reason for this high figure is the recent tendency to hide cars from public view.

Parking compounds and remote garage courts form ideal sheltered spaces in which children can play or vandals can strike, especially since such areas are rarely under the natural surveillance of the buildings they serve. It is generally agreed that distant spaces such as these should be avoided, as should the provision of parking next to footpaths. However, some sources argue that where both the parking component and the entrance are situated under natural surveillance then the fact that this is private space, not to be used as a play area, becomes apparent. Wherever situated, all garage doors should have strong bolts and locks.

Unsupervised, covered or multi-storey car parks have often proved unacceptable to residents and many have been demolished. Although many attempts to provide technological security systems to covered parking areas have been a failure, there are some examples where individual lock-up garages and the provision of a single controlled entrance to communal garages, using 'roll-over' gate access systems, have worked for several years, even in relatively high risk areas.

Ensure the casual surveillance of parked cars.

During 1981, residents in the 'Castles' section of the South Acton Estate in Ealing were consulted about the use of a garage block located in the centre of a grassed open space. The block had an upper floor of 52 garages above ground and a lower floor of 52 garages underground. Most of the upper floor was vandalized and few garages were in use. None of the lower floor garages were in use. The survey found that, if the garages were secured, residents would be willing to rent them at a slightly increased rental. Ealing Council introduced a card-operated electronic roll-over gate control access system, improved the fabric and rented the garages in 1982. They have been fully used since then, with few incidents of theft or damage.

5.4 EXTERNAL LIGHTING

Research in this country and America suggests that in certain circumstances improved external lighting can help to reduce crime levels and lessen the fear of crime. Effective lighting increases the potential offenders' feeling of exposure and improves the chances of identification and detection. Successful lighting also reassures, prevents accidents, aids orientation and provides a valuable amenity. It is important to ensure that lighting does not dazzle, nor should it create pockets of darkness since these can create additional problems.

It is important to take account of the type, intensity and location of lighting. Evenness of illumination is important and care should be taken to ensure that light fittings are arranged to obtain an even distibution over an area. Light thrown into people's faces helps identification at a distance, and is particularly important in areas such as underground car parks and pedestrian walkways. Lamps should therefore be placed along walls and not on ceilings.

To reduce crime problems, higher levels of planned uniform illumination are required than is currently the norm. However, intense floodlighting may well offer a deterrent, but can also create a harsh 'Colditz' effect which residents may find oppressive. It is important to provide a safe and attractive environment. Where there is a conflict of interest between vehicles and pedestrians, the needs of pedestrians should have priority. For example, tall monochromatic street lamps are suitable for roads but are likely to provide inadequate lighting for footpaths and may create shadows where pedestrians could be vulnerable.

The limited evidence from research suggests that 40% of night-time street crime occurs when lighting levels are at 5 lux or below (a lux is a measure of lighting: a typical side street has a level of about 2 lux at night and about 18 000 lux on a bright day). Only 3% of night-time street crime takes place when the lighting level is above 20 lux. Lighting levels of not less than 5 lux for most side streets, and not less than 15 for most estates and access routes would be appropriate.

Low pressure sodium lamps should be phased out in favour of high pressure lamps which are far less monochromatic and therefore aid colour rendition and recognition. Photoelectric cells are cheaper, easier to maintain and more reliable than time switches; and when they fail they tend to fail 'on'. Time-switched lamps can be inoperative for several weeks if there is a long

External lighting can help to reduce crime levels.

maintenance cycle. The type and location of fitting should be selected for ease of maintenance and replacement of bulb. As a general principle single fittings are unsatisfactory and multiple lights in the same area will provide a more constant level of protection.

Low energy, vandal resistant lighting needs to be fitted in entrance halls and corridors of multi-occupied blocks. Apart from increased effectiveness, revenue savings from reduced energy usage and damage will cover the cost of installation in three to four years. Some units contain replacement fittings which are automatically activated when a lamp fails.

Footpaths can be lit by lighting bollards. There are several types designed to be highly vandal resistant. These bollards can be sited within planted beds offering protection and creating a pleasant effect. However, whilst visually attractive, bollard lighting has the disadvantage that it does not illuminate to a sufficient height for an oncoming person to be fully seen and is not recommended as the only light source. Whenever possible lighting along footpaths should be combined with fittings associated with entrances. Even if the fittings by front doors are connected to the outdoor supplies they 'belong' to a particular property; not only is this inherently safer, but broken fittings will be replaced more rapidly.

5.5 LANDSCAPING

Landscaping plays an essential part in making an environment friendly and pleasant. However, planted areas are often poorly maintained or vandalized, and they can provide cover for dubious activities. Landscaping should not detract from pedestrians' visibility, nor should it create secluded areas for intruders to lurk.

Landscaping and planting associated with footpaths should reinforce security and as a general rule should not exceed 1 m where abutting pavements. Planting should be graded with taller plants next to walls, lower plants and shrubs adjacent to footpaths. Taller growing shrubs and trees should be avoided in areas which screen doorways, entrances and windows. Breaking and entering can be carried out with relative ease behind tall, dense planting. For the general security of premises, trees should not give concealment and so any in critical locations should be species without any branches below 1.5 m (for their own protection it is better if there are no branches below 2.4 m). The skillful planting of climbing plants may also prevent graffiti.

The appropriate selection of plant material is important within any scheme. Often financial restraints on landscape budgets do not allow for the use of larger, better established planting at the outset of a scheme, yet it has been shown that an initial additional outlay permitting the specification of stronger, better quality planting increases its chances of survival. A familiar sight in many public spaces is the sad and brutalized remains of young saplings. Planted in communal areas saplings rarely survive and the traditional methods of protecting them with wire cages or timber stakes are inadequate; if used they should generally be placed in gardens. The worst location for saplings is at the junction of several footpaths, sited within a flush tree grid. Money is better spent on fewer, more mature trees sited carefully away from the casual passer-by and possibly protected by other planting. The use of heavy standard (120–140 mm girth), extra heavy standard (140–160 mm girth) or even semi-mature trees (200–720 mm) will make it physically very difficult to snap off main growing stems. The involvement of the local community in the tree selection and planting programme can help to ensure the trees' survival.

Planting should be carefully specified, and any tendency for short cuts across beds can be deterred by the location of shrubs with prickly thorns, for example, gorse, berberis, holly or hawthorn. These can also be sited to protect more delicate foliage. This principle may be extended to provide protection for fencing or other landscaping elements that are liable to damage. A number of suppliers categorize their plant material which may include 'vandal recovery plants' or 'plants which discourage vandalism'.

The use of these types of planting does not necessarily guarantee success and can create a new set of problems such as snagging the clothing of passers-by, trapping litter, and minor injuries to young children. Certain types of shrubs, which if

Landscaping should not create secluded areas.

snapped or have stems broken off, will recover and indeed
readily grow new stems. The visual end result does, however,
tend to be one of mis-shaped, neglected plants.

It is also common sense to delay the installation of some
landscape features until the desire lines across the site have been
confirmed. Hard landscape details such as fencing and walls can
be used to physically deter pedestrian or vehicle movement
throughout a site. Soft landscape material alone cannot be used
as a physical barrier. Gravel paths and borders will constantly be
disturbed and should never be used. Deterrent surfaces can be
constructed using cobbles or large pebbles, but these must be
bedded into concrete for two-thirds of their own depth.

5.6 CASE STUDY OF THE DESIGN PROCESS

The Sandbrook Lane Estate in Moreton, on the outskirts of Wallasey, on the Wirral, Merseyside, was a typical development of the 1960s. There are four point blocks, each 15 storeys high, providing 85 one-, two-, and three-bedroom flats, with workshops, communal areas and ground level stores, some maisonettes, 12 shops, covered walkways and open grassed play areas. In all, the estate provided 900 new homes and the early tenants were happy, enjoying the modern facilities and splendid views.

In the early 1970s things started to go wrong. The original families moved out to larger accommodation, and were replaced by less stable tenants; the place became, in the words of one resident, like a 'transit camp'. The openness of the estate attracted vandals and drug addicts; a police sub-station closed and re-opened as an off-license; most of the shops closed as a result of continual break-ins. There were building fabric failures, and the sunken play areas, covered walkways and undercrofts were unused and became dangerous no-go areas. Even the views became obscured by motorway and other high rise developments. In the local government reorganization of 1974, Wallasey was swallowed up in the expanded and more distant Wirral Borough Council. The relationship between tenants and landlord was virtually non-existent. A community association forced some changes; improved public transport, a creche, an intercom system, re-housing for young families, but something more fundamental was needed.

In 1983, a new director of housing for Wirral was appointed and a programme launched to tackle problem estates, exploiting special funding that was available on Merseyside after the Toxteth riots. In 1985, Brock Carmichael Associates were appointed to look at a 1.5 acre site around one of the four blocks, comprising the tower block, 18 maisonettes and the shopping arcade, laid out round a 3-sided court containing car parking and a sunken play area. The architects proposed two options, both of which retained the tower block, with extensive renovations, including supplementary heating, new fire doors and smoke detection systems, window repairs, new lifts, a new escape stair, and conversion of three- to two-bedroom flats with internal and external redecoration to provide 85 flats for elderly people with a community centre and new shop units. The approved option involved the demolition of the low rise units and the construction of 22 new flats; half of which were for the disabled. Fundamental to the scheme was the formation of an enclosed development around the tower, reversing the previous concept of open access. A new court was formed by the tower block, the two storey new build flats and a community centre. Four shops were located in a new position, facing the street, rather than the court, which was landscaped, and contained car-parking in dispersed, broken up sections. The ground floor of the tower was cleared of stores to create a common room, a lobby area and a 'post-modern' porch.

The proposed scheme was presented to a general meeting of residents, and this was followed by a questionnaire, mostly to do with options for alternative accommodation. Elderly people were encouraged to stay, while families and single people were re-housed. The development appears open, but is highly secure. Close circuit television surveillance, linked to residents TV sets and monitored by receptionists/concierges ensures that any stranger to the site is quickly confronted. The elderly tenants, often more concerned about security than other social groups, find the high levels of security reassuring rather than intrusive. A combination of renovations and management initiatives, all specific to this particular site, seem to have reversed the process of decay. The scheme has received the 'Living in the City Award 1988'.

The other three tower blocks on the estate have also been segregated according to age groups: one for young singles, one for under 35s and one for under 50s.

FURTHER READING

British Standards Institute (1986) *BS 8220, British Standard Guide for Security of Buildings Against Crime: Part 1 Dwellings*, BSI, London.
Electricity Council (1987) *Essentials of Security Lighting*, Electricity Council.
Hellman, L. (1988) Paradise regained – Housing Renewal, Wirral, *Architects Journal*, **187** (31), 33–47.

Institute of Housing and RIBA (1989) *Safety and Security in Housing Design – A guide for action*, RIBA Publications Ltd, London.
Osborn, S. and Bright, J. (1989) *Crime Prevention and Community Safety: A practical guide for local authorities*, National Safe Neighbourhoods, London.

6

Design process – flats

6.1 COMMUNAL SPACE WITHIN BUILDINGS

Housing authorities have tried a variety of design and technical solutions to the problems of safety in communal areas. Some improvement schemes in tower blocks have created just one access point, opening into a supervised lobby. Others, in linear blocks with staircase access, have increased the number of access points and restricted the number of people using each one, constructing new entrance lobbies with stairwells serving only a few dwellings. Alternatively, access to dwellings can be restricted to one access point by a simple 'zone locking system'. Access to landings and balconies for non-residents is prevented by locked gates or doors designed for access/escape in emergencies only.

The use of common entrances should be avoided wherever possible and individual flat entrances should ideally be located at ground level. Where communal entrances are unavoidable, for example in multi-occupancy flats and maisonettes, they should be arranged so that as few residents as possible use each entrance. This enables residents to quickly get to know each other and develop natural protection (the principles of natural surveillance and neighbourhoods). A study of young single person schemes found that due to large numbers and diverse lifestyles, very few residents could identify more than a few of their neighbours. If there are more than four or five flats leading from a communal entrance then a controlled entry system will be required to guard against unauthorized access. Communal entrances should always be discrete, obviously for residents only and not through ways providing short cuts.

Problems of security and crime are often exacerbated where there are long access balconies and interconnecting walkways. Shortening the effective length of these access routes reduces the number of people using each entrance and may allow the successful introduction of phone entry systems. This can be achieved by demolishing walkways or by erecting permanent barriers. The horizontal or vertical 'partitioning' of blocks can create zones into which access is only possible with proximity cards or 'suited' keys. However, this is only likely to work if there are exceptionally good caretaking and management arrangements.

Any shared facilities which are provided (for example, drying areas or rubbish collection facilities) should be located within a secure area and in view of the dwellings they serve in order that they are protected by natural surveillance. Well lit, vandal resistant surfaces should be provided in this secure private area.

6.2 ENTRY-PHONES

Modern technology offers some opportunities for housing authorities to improve the security of their properties and the safety of their residents. However, in many cases, it is only effective in conjunction with on-site staff.

Phone entry systems have been installed in a wide range of blocks, and experience has shown that the smaller the number of dwellings served, the more likely that the systems will work. Once again, the key to their success seems to be the design of a system which is easily managed and maintained. In some blocks, the level of abuse and volume of traffic may be too much for any technology to withstand. In such circumstances, phone entry systems will need to be complemented by a block receptionist or concierge service. One option is for block entrance doors to remain open during the receptionist's hours of duty. Visitors report to the receptionist who can contact residents by intercom. When there is no receptionist cover, security would be achieved by the phone entry system alone. This would probably be between 1 am and 6 am, or for whatever period the traffic through the block is lightest.

The use of common entrances should be avoided.

In low crime areas, phone entry system can work without the need for human intervention in small or medium sized blocks serving up to 50 dwellings, providing there is regular checking and good maintenance. Phone entry systems often do not help ground-floor residents. Effective window and door security is often more important to residents on the ground floor.

6.3 CLOSED CIRCUIT TELEVISION

Closed circuit television (CCTV) involves the installation of video cameras in vandal resistant holdings at certain key points, such as lifts, lobbies, landings, parking and play areas, to enable activity to be monitored inside and outside blocks. Pictures from cameras continuously surveying areas where there is constant activity and movement need to be watched at all times to act as an effective deterrent. Pictures can be monitored by a concierge/receptionist or other security personnel. In areas where there is normally no regular activity movement detectors can be used, allowing cameras to switch on automatically to monitor any movement as it occurs. It is also possible to have instant

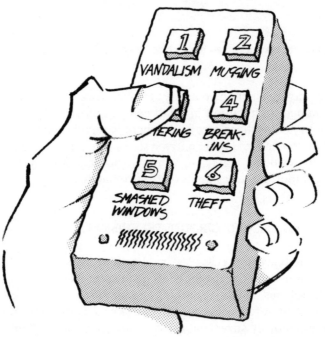

Closed circuit television.

freeze-frame and a print-out facility enabling the operative to locate an intruder and to obtain a still photograph for identification. Offenders, however, will not necessarily be deterred by cameras alone and camera lenses can easily be obscured unless very carefully sited.

Pictures from CCTV can also be monitored by residents on their own televisions, however this can cause more problems than it may solve. Residents' privacy may be abused. It is not always clear what residents should do if they see something suspicious, and legitimate strangers can be difficult to distinguish from intruders. It can also provide the resident burglar with the opportunity to survey the activities of other residents.

Full consultation with residents about the introduction of CCTV is essential. It may be welcomed in some situations, but considered oppressive in others. There may be understandable concern about the confidentiality of recorded material and there are obvious implications for civil liberties.

6.4 EXAMPLES OF INTEGRATED RECEPTIONISTS/ TECHNOLOGY SYSTEMS

Phone entry and CCTV systems are access control systems not security systems. They may form part of a security package, if coupled with block receptionists, television surveillance or strengthened front doors. In most cases, reliance should not be placed on technological measures alone to improve security. It may be vandalized or stolen, and will not necessarily reduce crime or make people feel safer. In multi-storey blocks, the level of security given to individual dwellings should depend on the level of risk and adequacy of security at the block entrance and in the communal areas. Correct assessment of the requirements of each block is essential to identify appropriate individual and collective security measures and the right combination of design, management and technological approaches. The following examples indicate the need to take such an integrated approach combining design improvements, new reception systems and suitable technology.

On the Lisson Green Estate in Westminster, it has been

shown that a reduction in robberies was associated with blocking off the access to the walkways by a phone entry system rather than the subsequent, more expensive, walkway removal programme. However, on the Chalkhill Estate in the London Borough of Brent, the use of entry-phones and CCTV was tried in two phases of improvements, with limited success. In 1980 extensive improvements were carried out to access ways, and walkways were divided into sections by security doors controlled by entry phone systems, restricting access to those residents who lived on that section. The first phase of improvements had very limited success due to ill-conceived design and poor planning. There had been little consultation with tenants, and the security doors were resented (and removed) when people found routes they had used for years were suddenly blocked off. The doors had fundamental weaknesses and were easily damaged and prevented from working effectively. The second improvement phase was only applied to two blocks and this time changes were far more extensive and costly. They included the removal of walkways, the creation of new lobby areas and the provision of entry phones and CCTV surveillance. Although these changes have proved effective in the improved blocks, considerable resentment has been caused on the rest of the estate as there is little likelihood of the scheme being extended.

Barking and Dagenham Borough Council's Housing Department has undertaken an ambitious re-design scheme to link three neighbouring 15 storey tower blocks through a central reception area. The key feature of this scheme is the construction of a new reception building with covered walkways leading to the blocks. The decision to adopt this scheme followed a survey and consultation process organized by the Safe Neighbourhoods Unit. A previous attempt to improve security in 1985 by installing phone-entry controlled doors and camera surveillance was repeatedly vandalized and rarely in operation. The SNU proposed a three phase strategy:

1. a purpose built and permanently staffed reception area;
2. environmental improvements;
3. a community centre added to the reception area.

The physical proximity of the three blocks meant that it was possible to link them via enclosed walkways to a main reception area at the centre of the development. This enables one receptionist to control access to all the blocks and means that all visitors have to pass through one reception area. Although there is a high capital cost involved, the day to day running costs should be lower than some receptionist or concierge schemes, since one team of receptionists can control three blocks. The design of the scheme reduces the reliance on technology for monitoring block access and this may also prove economical in the long-term. There will be cameras for entrances and lifts and phone entry systems, but these will be wired via the reception area.

Sheffield City Council's Housing Department has begun to upgrade a very large deck access estate in the city, involving the enclosure and partitioning of some decks, phone/key entry zone control, and receptionists at zone entrances. The estate comprises two long blocks each up to 12 storeys in height and meandering across a sloping site. They are linked by a set of vertically stacked bridges. The unusual features of Sheffield's approach is the division of linked blocks and the redesign of blocks to encourage tenant control over their immediate surroundings. The improvements consist of the fitting of improved doors and security locks to main entrances of all private dwellings and the enclosing of some decks with glazing to turn them into corridors. Where decks connect to adjacent blocks, locked doors are being installed, for which only tennants of the secured blocks will have keys. The decks are further partitioned with self-closing doors to encourage a sense of 'ownership' of the sections of the decks by small groups of neighbouring tennants. Seating is also installed in these partitioned areas and lighting in all access routes is being improved. The only common entrance accessible for visitors will have a front door controlled by a receptionist, leading to a reception area and improved lifts.

Southchurch Court is a single tower block built in 1969 on the Clifton Estate in Nottingham. It includes 96 one-bedroom and 34 two-bedroom flats. The block was isolated and surrounded by grass, and although there was a single main entrance many people used the five fire doors. It suffered from a high level of damage and crime, and was hard to let. Improvements were made in late 1986 and early 1987 and crime levels in the block dropped dramatically, with vandalism almost disappearing. The building is no longer hard to let and half of the occupants are fairly long stay.

The improvements included closed circuit television cameras monitored by 24hr 'block patrollers'. The in-fill of the space between pilloti at ground level to form store rooms for housing services, offices for the 'block patrollers' and the housing department, and a community room. The fire doors were fitted with alarms to stop them being used as alternative entrances. New fencing (1800 mm high) was put up around the edge of the plot with some planting along the fencing. New footpaths were laid across the plot following the desire lines. new external lighting was installed. Although the main door had to be fitted with an automatic opening device triggered by a photo-electric cell, due to wind damage, there was no upgrading of the door ironmongery on individual flats. The 'block patrollers' (their name for what other authorities call concierges or receptionists) are liked by the residents and they are often asked to take in parcels or keep keys for flats. The emergency switches in the flats linked to the block controller also serve a 999 function.

FURTHER READING

Bright, J. *et al.* (1985) *After Entry Phones: Improving management and security in multi-storey blocks*, NACRO Safe Neighbourhoods Unit, London.

British Standards Institute, (1986) *BS 8220, British Standard Guide for Security of Buildings Against Crime: Part 1 Dwellings*, BSI, London.

Crouch, S. (1989) *Practical Guide to Improving Timber Entrance Door Security*, Safe Neighbourhoods Advisory Service, London.

Crouch, S. (1989) *Practical Guide to Improving Window Security*, Safe Neighbourhoods Advisory Service, London.

Crouch, S. (1989) *Practical Guide to Improved Fixing Methods*, Safe Neighbourhoods Advisory Service, London.

Crouch, S. (1989) *Practical Guide to Improving Emergency Exit Door Security*, Safe Neighbourhoods Advisory Service, London.

Crouch, S. (1990) *Practical Guide to Improving Doors to Flats in Multi-storey Blocks*, Safe Neighbourhoods Advisory Service, London.

Crouch, S. (1990) *Practical Guide to Improving the Security of Flat Conversions*, Safe Neighbourhoods Advisory Service, London.

Cummings, N. (1987) *Security: The comprehensive guide to equipment selection and installation*, Architectural Press Ltd, London.

Institute of Housing and RIBA (1989) *Safety and Security in Housing Design – A Guide for Action*, RIBA Publications Ltd, London.

Osborn, S. and Bright, J. (1989) *Crime Prevention and Community Safety: A practical guide for local authorities*, National Safe Neighbourhoods, London.

7 Design process – houses

7.1 LAYOUT

When designing the layout of a new housing development the first three principles outlined in Chapter 3 are critical. They can be regarded as objectives which the architect should be seeking to achieve.

1. Maximize the opportunities for natural or passive surveillance of both dwellings and their surrounding public spaces.
2. Create a sense of neighbourhood, by limiting the number of access points and routes into and through a neighbourhood.
3. Indicate clearly the boundaries between public and private space, encouraging a sense of ownership and responsibility.

However, given such opposing theories of security design as those outlined in Chapter 2, it is hardly surprising that two distinctly different design trends to satisfy these objectives can be identified. These relate in particular to the discussion of what constitutes a neighbourhood.

The first school of thought suggests the use of culs-de-sac or loop roads as the appropriate design solution. Such layouts, with dwellings facing each other, provide good natural surveillance. Restricting through traffic allows the street to be used as a communal space. This may encourage a sense of ownership and enable residents to readily identify each other and notice intruders or strangers. The use of culs-de-sac does provide better surveillance at the front of the dwellings, but it can create larger rear areas that are hidden from view. Whilst some sources argue that culs-de-sac and restricted estate roads are useful designs to increase both the security of the dwelling and the safety of the street users, others disagree. The opportunities for casual

Culs-de-sac can deter.

surveillance from passing cars or by pedestrians will be reduced, and it can be argued that such road layouts are a bogus safety factor since they teach children that roads are safe to play on. Children reared on normal roads are taught kerb drill from an early age and are not lulled into a false sense of security.

The second school of thought proposes through roads as the most appropriate design solution, providing that some measures are taken to safeguard the residents by ensuring that both vehicular speed and volume is reduced, for example, by incorporating 'traffic calming' measures such as those used in the Woonerf system in Holland. It is argued that through traffic encourages street life and that a busy street, especially one with pedestrians and people using the street as an extension of their semi-private space, ensures constant surveillance and thus security. 'Traffic calming' is a design-based approach to managing traffic in residential areas, shopping areas and on main roads. It aims to significantly reduce the dominance of motor traffic in many urban areas, and improve road safety and the appearance of the street through the comprehensive introduction of features designed to regulate the flow of traffic. These should emphasize to motorists the need to restrict their speed and/or take appropriate care whilst taking full account of the particular needs of pedestrians, cyclists and wheelchair users. Successful traffic calming measures are, in themselves, an environmental improvement, for example, they could be designed in order to increase the amount of greenery in the area.

Although these different theoretical approaches to the problem result in quite different design solutions, they are not necessarily contradictory. Depending on the site, a combination of these measures, such as through roads and culs-de-sac, could be a feasible option.

7.2 PRIVATE SPACE

Boundaries do not necessarily have to be physical entities, but they should provide a clear demarcation between private and public space. For example, different colours and textures of surfacing materials can be used to differentiate between public and private footpaths. Alternatively a definite barrier or narrowed access creating a gateway symbolizes entry to the non-public area. Although some boundaries may only need to be of a token nature in some close housing situations, boundary protection will be required where semi-private space abuts public space and where vulnerable groups, such as the elderly need such protection to alleviate the fear of crime.

If possible, all ground floor dwellings should have a front garden and the design should ensure that individual tenancy/ ownership is readily identifiable. It is suggested that the front garden should provide a semi-private buffer zone between the private space of the dwelling and the public space of the pavement; the community recognizes that this belongs to the occupants, so anyone who enters but does not knock on the front door is seen as behaving suspiciously.

Waist high walls should follow the exact frontage line between the garden and the pavement, giving a clear, unambiguous barrier between public and semi-private space. High walls create facelessness and obstruct surveillance, whilst low walls or open rails do not control either animals or children. The front wall can be a vital learning aid for children to help them distinguish

Traffic calming measures.

between public and private space (presumably it serves the same function for adults).

Side boundaries between private gardens could have high fences for the first 2–3 m nearest the house, giving privacy to the ground floor. The remaining length of the side fence could be lower to allow natural surveillance of surrounding dwellings. Where side boundaries are located alongside roads, paths or open ground particular care should be taken to form a secure private area. The addition of a trellis on top of walls and fences and the provision of prickly shrubs can act as a further deterrent.

The layout should be designed or modified to avoid the need for the dwellings and their private areas to be entered by strangers and by persons making deliveries, collections or taking meter readings. Meters should be located where they can be read without the need to enter the secure part of the building. They should also be sited where the reader is in clear view of the residents; there have been instances of burglars disconnecting electricity at external meters as a way of checking whether or not premises are occupied.

There should be no way of gaining access from the front to the rear of the dwelling. Access to the rear should be via full height locked gates or through the garage. Adjacent houses should, where possible, present an unbroken façade, any gaps allow intruders to gain access to the more vulnerable rear of the house. This may only be viable in high density housing. Where a path is provided from the front to the rear of the dwelling, access should be restricted by the provision of a stout gate, not readily climbed, and secured by locks and bolts which cannot be reached from the front. Such gates should be located as near as possible to the building line so they are in view of the neighbours.

The rear buffer area or garden should have a stout fence (1.8 m high is generally recommended). Whilst some literature advocates the provision of a strong gate to allow rear access, this is not generally considered to be a viable option. Instead, a layout is recommended which enables houses to back onto the rear of another dwelling. Any access to the rear fence, for example if it abutted open land or a footpath, may enable an intruder to gain access regardless of the fence height. Once over the fence the intruder has gained cover and access to the dwelling. The only way to avoid this is to prevent the intruder gaining access to the fence.

The layout should try to avoid unsecured rear gardens that back onto footpaths or common ground. Where possible, rear garden areas should be designed to face and adjoin each other so they provide their own protection against entry. Particular care should be taken where dwellings abut open spaces (railway embankments, industrial estates, common land, park land). Access to private areas from such open spaces should be deterred by providing high robust fences which are difficult to climb. Planting prickly shrubs can act as a further deterrent and protect fences from access, graffiti and damage.

7.3 INDIVIDUAL DWELLINGS

It is best if residents can see clearly what is happening outside their homes, not only to detect intruders in their own 'private' space, or interference with their own cars, but also to keep a watchful eye on their neighbours' dwellings and vehicles. Projections on the façades of the dwelling which impede the line of vision should therefore be carefully considered. Window design is an important factor when considering how to provide good lines of natural surveillance at the front of ground floor units. Oriel or bay windows are pleasing design features and also provide good lines of surveillance. Small windows, or windows above eye level should be avoided at the front of ground floor dwellings, as should the use of beaded, frosted or patterned glass. Recessed doors can provide cover for the would-be intruder and should therefore be avoided.

Entrances should not be placed in isolation as this may make them vulnerable, but neither should they be concentrated in one area as this may leave large areas of blank wall. A porch desirable as a weather shelter to entrances could hide intruders and facilitate the use of force on the entrance door. In such circumstances glass which could be broken to reach locks should be avoided and the door and its frame, fixings, hinges and locks should be strong.

Designers should avoid including any feature which could be used as a ladder to gain access to upper floor entry points. For example, the position of rubbish bins and fuel stores should be carefully considered, and attention should be paid to the location of boundary walls, flat roofs, balconies, drainpipes and porches. Projections and recesses are often used to add aesthetic interest to large housing blocks. Unfortunately, they may also act as stepping stones and hiding places for people intent on committing crime. Generally speaking, from a security point of view, the first 2.5 m from ground level of a building's elevation should have a reasonably smooth 'coastline'. This will maximize

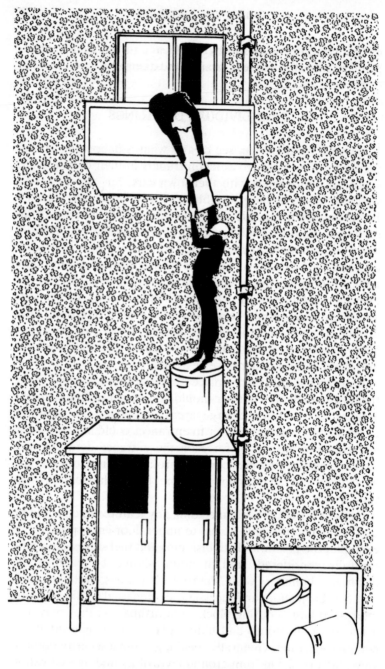

Any feature which could be used as a ladder.

natural surveillance and minimize footholds for illegal access. Similarly, downpipes and gutters have to be carefully detailed to avoid their use as climbing aids for the burglar or vandal. If re-design and relocation are not feasible, then protruding metal barriers or non-setting paint may have to be used, as a last resort, in particularly vulnerable locations.

Architects need to recognize the nature of burglary before deciding on the type of measure to be used. Most burglary is opportunist and relatively modest expenditure can prevent a high proportion of incidents. The advent of battery power tools means that even very expensive improvements are unlikely to deter the small number of professionals and therefore expensive hardware is of limited value.

In terraced houses or tenement blocks roof voids and large ducting areas can sometimes be used as access routes for burglary. Service hatches for such spaces need to be well secured, and the spaces themselves need to be securely partitioned as far as possible. All possible means of access to the dwelling need to be identified and, if possible, strengthened.

Niddrie in Edinburgh consists of numerous four storey walk-up blocks built in the 1930s with four flats accessible from each landing. Tenants living in the top flats of the blocks would sometimes come home to find gaping holes in their ceilings and all their valuables gone. Ingenious burglars would climb the common stair, force the service hatch in the ceiling of the top landing, and then wander through the pitched roof void. They could then literally drop into somebody's living room and remove the items they wanted via the front door. The council eventually installed entryphones at the main entrance to each block, but because there were so many families housed there most of the entrance doors were wedged open so that children could play inside and outside.

7.4 TARGET HARDENING

As a general principle, the security value of any door or window is dependant on the type and construction, the strength and reliability of hardware locking mechanisms, the strength and fixing of frames, the adequacy of any glazing and the degree of visibility. Glazed panels should not be located near locks. If there is no alternative to using glazing next to the door then door frames and hinges need to be extra strong. Such glazing should be shatter-proof in this location.

Many housing estates have poorly constructed doors and frames. It is not usually worthwhile to add locks and bolts in these circumstances without replacing the doors and frames as well. The same is true for poorly constructed or rotting window frames. Authorities unable to afford the cost of a general programme of upgrading doors and windows may consider introducing a partial programme, by replacing doors and windows with better quality equivalents as and when they are in need of repair. Local authorities may also consider phasing improvements in security provision by concentrating resources on burglary victims. A particular problem for houses is the security arrangements provided for enclosed porches. Ideally, the outer porch door should be the focus for security hardware. If the porch door is not secure, it allows easy entry and cover for intruders to work on the dwelling door.

Physical security measures will often be a key element in any crime prevention strategy. Whether for individual dwellings or large multi-storey blocks, it is important for equipment to be well designed and sufficiently robust to withstand heavy use and normal levels of abuse. Strength and reliability are particularly important where the location does not allow a high degree of public surveillance. Uniformly robust components and hardware should be specified. If it is intended to fit alarm systems to individual dwellings on an estate, it is better to fit a variety of different types; once the weaknesses of a particular system have been identified, the system is no longer effective and the whole estate could be at risk.

7.5 CASE STUDY OF THE DESIGN PROCESS

The Kirkholt housing estate is situated on the southern fringe of Rochdale. The bulk of the estate was built between 1948 and 1953 and comprises some 200 units providing housing for

Glass panels should not be located near locks.

approximately 7000 people. Unemployment is relatively high (average 16%, 1988) and the estate exhibits a range of social problems.

The estate was selected by the Department of the Environment for a Priority Estates Project (PEP) in 1985. PEP status has enabled Rochdale Metropolitan Borough Housing Department to carry out an ambitious programme of improvement work focusing mainly on a 'warm and dry' project to provide the dwellings with central heating. This upgrading took place in 1988/9 and also covered replacement doors, mortice locks and window locks.

Even before the 'warm and dry' scheme, work had begun in order to reduce crime, and in particular burglary, on the estate. The original programme concentrated on dwellings which had been the subject of more than one burglary and consisted of a series of stages.

1. Survey by community programme workers into the incidence of crime on the estate.
2. Immediate remedial measures to any house that was burgled, with a joiner sent to repair doors and replace locks. This was to tackle the problem of repeat burglaries.
3. Meters changed in vulnerable houses to non-cash type.
4. The establishment of 'cocoons'; victim support networks to

protect areas at particular risk. These later merged to form 'Home Watch' groups.

5. The offer of post-coding for valuables.
6. The establishment of a local victim support scheme.

Other design improvements on the estate cover the fences, lighting, garages, footpaths and landscaping. Such an extensive programme of improvement has required good co-ordination between the housing and both technical services and highways departments of the local authority.

Fences have been improved at both the front and rear of dwellings. These are now normally 3 ft high and of timber with 2 horizontal wire strands to strengthen them. On occasion the height at the rear has been raised to 4 ft and in special cases wire mesh is used.

The level of lighting within the estate has been dramatically improved with the full support of the residents. This has been done in a series of stages with the first priority being elderly peoples' accommodation, then flats and then shared areas (quadrangles and courtyards). Bulkhead lights have also been fitted over entrances and additional lighting provided for footpaths within the estate.

The estate has a below average level of car ownership and many of the garages were not being used. The council, therefore, adopted a policy of either repairing and letting, or demolishing the garages. The ones repaired were mainly those in in-fill locations or on street corners. Those demolished were mainly in large groups (20 plus units) or in concealed locations. In total about one third of the stock was demolished (in excess of 100 units). One such cleared garage site is now being used as a playground. There is an unofficial trend for the development of car hardstandings immediately in front of dwellings, and it is recognized that this may be the long-term solution.

There have been no major changes to the pattern of pedestrian footpaths, but a number of unofficial desire lines have been recognized and made up as proper footpaths.

The estate has a large amount of open land and in an attempt to develop this most effectively a study was undertaken by the Oldham and Rochdale Groundwork Trust leading to the appointment of an environmental project officer. Care is being taken to use low maintenance planting and to avoid the creation of potential hiding places. Two new play areas are under development on the estate. There are a lot of elderly and single parent families on the estate, and there is little prospect of extending the amount of land under individual control. One of the severe problems is where tenants have 'drawn back' the boundaries of their territory and areas of unclaimed land have developed.

These measures appear to have been extremely successful and there has been a 78% reduction in burglaries (comparing the first 8 months of 1986 with the first 8 months of 1989). There is also no evidence of a significant displacement of crime to adjoining estates.

FURTHER READING

Bennett, G., Noble, J. and Jenks, M. (1984) *More than Just a Road*, Information Directorate, DoE.

British Standards Institute (1986) *BS 8220, British Standard Guide for Security of Buildings Against Crime: Part 1 Dwellings*, BSI, London.

Crouch, S. (1989) *Practical Guide to Improving Timber Entrance Door Security*, Safe Neighbourhoods Advisory Service, London.

Crouch, S. (1989) *Practical Guide to Improving Window Security*, Safe Neighbourhoods Advisory Service, London.

Crouch, S. (1989) *Practical Guide to Improved Fixing Methods*, Safe Neighbourhoods Advisory Service, London.

Crouch, S. (1989) *Practical Guide to Improving Emergency Exit Door Security*, Safe Neighbourhoods Advisory Service, London.

Department of Transport (1987) *Measures to Control Traffic for the Benefit of Residents, Pedestrians and Cyclists*, Traffic Advisory Unit Leaflet 1/87 Department of Transport, London.

Institute of Housing and RIBA (1989) *Safety and Security in Housing Design – A Guide for Action*, RIBA Publications Ltd, London.

National House-Building Council, (NHBC) (1986) *Guidance on how the Security of New Homes can be Improved*, NHBC,

Osborn, S. and Bright, J. (1989) *Crime Prevention and Community Safety; A practical guide for local authorities*, National Safe Neighbourhoods, London.

8

Construction process

This chapter is mainly concerned with the construction process in the upgrading of existing estates. However, many of the topics covered are also relevant in the construction of new housing developments.

8.1 PLANNING AND PROGRAMMING THE WORK

Once the specific problems of an estate have been identified and the improvement measures decided upon, it is essential that any programme of work is carefully planned in a series of 'self contained' phases. There are two reasons for this. Firstly, many housing authorities face uncertainties over future funding, and it is important that any phase of work undertaken is independently effective. Secondly, any initiatives depend to a great extent on the goodwill and co-operation of residents. If a lengthy programme seems to be providing no more than continual disruption, the goodwill of residents will quickly evaporate.

It may be necessary to make modifications to the design during the construction process, and it is important to be prepared to make any essential changes in response to feedback from residents. If the work has been planned in phases it is important to recognize the effects of any modifications on future stages of work. The need for modifications may only become apparent after a trial period of use, or as circumstances on the estate change. Again consultation with residents is the most effective way to identify areas where changes need to be made.

8.2 SPECIFICATION AND QUALITY CONTROL

The specification of materials needs to be given careful consideration and they should be robust and easily maintained and replaced. Throughout the construction process it is essential to carry out checks to ensure that the contractors are actually using the specified materials, and that any new features or security measures are correctly and securely installed. Design features that are in areas of public use obviously need to be especially robust, and will quickly fail if they have been poorly constructed or incorrectly installed. The same is true of any target hardening measures fitted to individual dwellings. The strongest of locks will not act as a deterrent if they are incorrectly fitted or if the door and window frames are rotten or insubstantial.

There have been, in the past, some 'improvements' which have been of actual assistance to burglars. On one tower block refurbishment the automatically triggered porch lighting had been designed to switch itself on as people approached the building. However, it was wired in reverse, so that it switched itself off as soon as anyone entered, plunging the entrance lobby into darkness. On another development the spyholes in the front doors were installed the wrong way round. This allowed outsiders to look into each flat as they walked along the corridor, but prevented householders from seeing out.

8.3 SITE SECURITY AND SAFETY

Security problems may well increase during the construction period. Apart from the obvious opportunities for theft of materials and tools, strangers will be less conspicuous when building workers have access to an estate as a whole, and also to individual dwellings.

If scaffolding is erected around buildings which remain occupied during refurbishment, extra precautions should be taken. The occupiers should be advised of their increased vulnerability and, where appropriate, should be offered free installation of window locks and other security aids. Outside working hours the contractor should ensure that unauthorized

Site security.

access is prevented by removing or chaining ladders, fixing sheet metal and overhangs at key points and installing security lighting.

Building sites are often magnets for bored youngsters and it is therefore most important to secure equipment and materials that can be misused. Rubble and inflammable waste should be removed as quickly as possible from any areas to which the public have access. Builders' materials, equipment and waste may be used as aids to crime and vandalism if they are not properly secured. Rubble can provide ammunition to break windows. Paint and cement can become childrens' 'play' materials. Timber stock and waste can be used for starting fires.

If outside contractors are used, the provision of on-site security and a secure contractor's compound should be part of the terms of contract. If a council or housing association use their own work force, security requirements should be considered as part of the plan of work. The co-operation of residents is essential.

Site security measures should include a 2.4 m perimeter fence topped with at least one strand of barbed wire and with view slots at eye level. The site hut should be elevated for a view over the site and for load inspection. There should be at least a 915 mm gap between the site fence and the site hut. The door and shell of the site hut should be attack resistant (e.g. 18 mm ply), and the roof should be of the same strength as the walls. There needs to be laminated glass or polycarbonate windows in the site hut, or failing that, lift off or hinged grills or panels locking over the windows. There should be deadlocks to doors on site huts.

Security lighting needs to be elevated for night 'natural', or 'formal' surveillance. Plant, vehicles, pumps, etc. need to be immobilized at night with keys or vital parts secured in a key box in the site hut. All tools should be kept in secure lockers and loose components secured in 'immovable' amounts and/or to ground stakes. Plant and equipment needs to be clearly and permanently marked and secured if too large to be put away.

8.4 HAND-OVER AND EVALUATION

In the period between completion of work and hand-over there is risk of damage to, or theft from, individual dwellings. A house can be stripped and gutted in a matter of hours. Residents must be installed in their new homes as quickly as possible after completion, to avoid properties standing empty. If this is not practical then arrangements must be made for security provision. The dwellings or communal facilities must be quickly handed over to those who will be responsible for them.

On moving in, residents must be made aware of how any security installations, from window locks to alarm systems, work; one reason why many security measures fail is simply because they are not used correctly, or not used at all.

In terms of effective estate redesign, the hand-over after completion of works should not be the end of the story: where residents have been moved out temporarily, it is only after they have moved back into their homes and resumed their normal daily life that it is possible to evaluate the effectiveness of improvements. It may also be some time before the long term value of some aspects of the redesign can be fully gauged. There are many examples of estates which have been given cosmetic improvements only to revert to their former decay within a couple of years. In order to inform future development work and to optimize existing upgrades, it is important to undertake periodic evaluations of work already completed. So often this is omitted from contracts and development programmes, with the result that lessons are not learnt and costly mistakes are repeated.

Evaluation should be threefold. Firstly, a technical appraisal of the maintenance requirements and durability of improvements. Secondly, user satisfaction surveys (and analysis of data

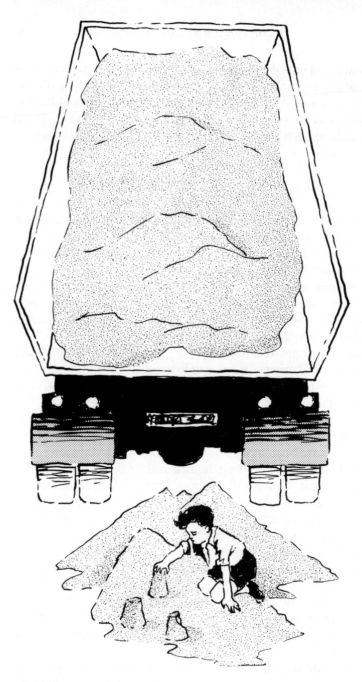

Site safety.

such as crime figures). Finally, an estimate of likely lettings (and the turnover of tenants). Such evaluations can provide an informed base on which to refine existing developments, and resources need to be made available for this to happen. Some estates have such severe problems that they will need repeated interventions. In these cases a one-off upgrade with no evaluation can be worse than useless.

Conclusion

To suggest that better design and layout alone can offer solutions to the problems of crime and security on new and existing housing developments is to ignore a whole range of social and economic factors which can affect the levels of crime in a particular area. Defensive design has a role in crime prevention, but factors such as unemployment, poverty, social stress and bad management simply cannot be designed out. A comprehensive approach must be taken to community safety which will include designing to deter and sensitive management policies.

On large public sector estates, residents rarely identify crime as their only problem, even in areas with high crime rates: unemployment, housing conditions or youth provision are usually cited as major concerns, although crime prevention is usually high on residents' lists of priorities. Local authorities can respond to these wider issues by providing opportunities for residents to be involved in decision-making by promoting a broad range of community facilities, by giving higher priority to youth and play provision and by responding, where they can, to local employment needs. Strengthening communities in this way can lead to an increase in the sort of informal community controls necessary to maintain a 'natural level of order' that will deter antisocial behaviour and petty offending. Current work on community safety emphasizes that design has to be reconciled with a number of other factors, crucial amongst which may be residents' involvement in local management and decision-making and the quality of neighbourhood services. Even more important may be the mix of residents, in particular the ratio of children to adults. Even if the theories of architectural determinists are totally correct, design solutions alone may be costly and slow to implement and difficult to reverse. Given the great pressure to reduce crime in public housing projects, officials must resist the temptation to go for quick and visible tactics such as evicting difficult tenants, introducing security patrols and fitting more locks. Unless a comprehensive community safety approach is taken which integrates social ameliorations and management improvements, energy and resources will be wasted. Design has its part to play in crime prevention, but it is unlikely to be the whole solution.

In the private sector, an important reason for including security measures at the design stage is that it is cheaper than trying to 'bolt-on' security later, and the options available at this stage will provide more effective and comprehensive cover than measures added later. As the public become increasingly aware of the importance of security in design, through such measures as the recent Government campaign to raise security consciousness and encourage informal policing by schemes like the Neighbourhood Watch, so security measures will increasingly become a selling point. It is at present a buyers' market, so these factors are beginning to have an effect. This growing demand is now being harnessed in the south-east of England by the police authorities 'Secured by Design' initiative where private builders can gain certificates for their developments by following certain principles.

Security is only one of many factors which need to be considered when designing housing. It should not be the main aim, but it should perhaps be given greater priority than at present. Designing to deter does not necessarily detract from, nor require drastic changes in, building form or site layout, provided it is considered at the design stage.

Videos

To accompany the original working papers, which gave rise to this book, two videos were produced. The first, 'Safe as Houses', was launched in 1988 and considers crime prevention through the design and layout of new housing estates. The second, 'Safer Neighbourhoods' (1989), examines the essential issues and processes which architects, planners and housing managers must consider when seeking to redesign housing developments to reduce crime and improve community safety. Examples of good and bad practice are illustrated in both videos, and other factors beyond design which also affect security are mentioned.

These videos have been made by CERCI Communications in conjunction with the Institute of Advanced Architectural Studies and the Safe Neighbourhoods Unit. They are in VHS format and have a running time of 17 and 35 minutes respectively.

'Safe as Houses' is available from:
CERCI Communications,
19 Store Street,
London WC1E 7BT.

'Safer Neighbourhoods' is available from:
The Safe Neighbourhoods Unit,
1st Floor,
485–7 Bethnal Green Road,
London E2 9QH.

Bibliography

BOOKS

Appleyard, D. (1981) *Liveable Streets*, University of California Press Ltd, London.

Barty, E., White, D. and Burall, P. (1980) *Safety and Security in the Home*, Design Council, London.

Barnard, R. L. (1981) *Intrusion Detection Systems, Principles of Operation and Application*, Butterworth.

Bennett, T. and Wright, R. (1984) *Burglars on Burglary, Prevention and the Offender*, Gower.

Brantingham (eds) (1981) *Environmental Criminology*, Sage, California.

British Standards Institute (1986) *BS 8220, British Standard Guide for Security of Buildings Against Crime: Part 1 Dwellings*, London.

Bugg, D. E. and Bridges, C. (1974) *Burglary Protection and Insurance Surveys*, Stone and Cox,

Capel, V. (1979) *Burglar Alarm Systems*, Newnes Technical Books, Butterworths,

Coleman, A. (1985) *Utopia on Trial*, Hilary Shipman, London.

Cummings, N. (1987) *Security: The comprehensive guide to equipment selection and installation*, Architectural Press Ltd, London.

Davidson, R. W. (1981) *Crime and Environment*, Croom Helm, London.

Djaafar, Daara (1987) *Problem Housing Estates: A study of conflicting claims about the causes*, MPhil, Department of Architecture, Oxford Polytechnic, Oxford.

Elliot, M. (1986) *Keeping Safe – A Practical Guide to Talking with Children*, Bedford Square Press, National Council for Voluntary Organisations.

Essex County Council (1973) *Essex Design Guide for Residential Areas*, Anchor Press Ltd,

Gigliotti, R. and Jason, R. (1984) *Security Design for Maximum Protection*, Butterworth,

Greater London Council (1978) *An Introduction to Housing Layout*, Architectural Press Ltd, London.

Hammer, J. and Saunders, S. (1984) *Well Founded Fear – A Community Study of Violence to Women*, Hutchinson,

Healy, R. (1983)*Design for Security*, 2nd edn, John Wiley and Sons, Chichester.

Hopf, P. S. (1979) *Handbook of Building Security Planning and Design*, McGraw-Hill,

Institute of Housing and RIBA (1988) *Tenant Participation in Housing Design*, RIBA Publications Limited, London.

Institute of Housing and RIBA (1989) *Safety and Security – A Guide for Action*, RIBA Publications Limited, London.

Jacobs, J. (1961) *The Death and Life of Great American Cities*, Jonathan Cape, London. (Also published by Penguin Books Ltd, 1965.)

Lawrence, R. J. (1987) *Housing, Dwellings and Homes; Design Theory, Research and Practice*, John Wiley and Sons, New York.

Lea, J. and Young, J. (1984) *What is to be done about Law and Order?*, Penguin Books Ltd, Harmondsworth.

Maguire, M. and Bennett, T. *Burglary in Dwellings*, Gower.

Marsh, P. (1985) *Security in Buildings*, Construction Press.

Matrix (1984) *Making Space: Women and the man-made environment*, Pluto Press.

Newman, O. (1972) *Defensible Space: People and design in the violent city*, Macmillan, New York.

Pearson, G. (1983) *Hooligan: A history of respectable fears*, Macmillan, London.

Power, A. (1987) *Property Before People: The management of twentieth century council housing*, Allen and Unwin.

Poyner, B. (1983) *Design Against Crime: Beyond defensible space*, Butterworths.

Rogers, M. R. *et al.* (1989) *Quality of Life in Britain's Intermediate Cities*, University of Glasgow, Glasgow.

Shapland, J. and Vagg, J. (1988) *Policing by the Public*, Routledge, London.

Sinnott, R. (1985) *Safety and Security in Building Design*, Collins.

Sykes, J. (ed.) (1979) *Designing Against Vandalism*, The Design Council, London.

Teymeur, Markus, Woolley, (eds) (1988) *Rehumanising Housing*, Butterworth.

Traini, R. (1984) *Home Security and Protection*, Willow Books, Collins.

Underwood, G. (1984) *The Security of Buildings*, Architectural Press Ltd, London.

Walsh, D. (1980) *Break-ins, Burglary from Private Houses*, Constable.

Warren, F. (1988) *The design of purpose built, public sector housing provision for young single people*, PhD Thesis, Department of Architecture, Oxford Polytechnic.

Wright, K. G. (1972) *Cost Effective Security*, McGraw Hill.

GOVERNMENT PUBLICATIONS

Audit Commission (1986) *Improving House Maintenance*, HMSO, London.

Bennett, G., Noble, J. and Jenks, M. (1984) *More than Just a Road*, Information Directorate, Department of the Environment, London.

Clarke, R. V. G. (ed.) (1978) *Tackling Vandalism*, Home Office Research Study No 47, HMSO, London.

Clarke, R. V. G. and Mayhew, P. (1980) *Designing Out Crime*, HMSO, London.

Department of the Environment (1986/87) *The Urban Programme, Action for Cities, Building on Initiative*, HMSO, London.

Department of the Environment (1989) *Handbook of Estate Improvement: Volume 1 Guidance on Option Appraisal*, HMSO, London.

Department of Transport (1987) *Measures to Control Traffic for the Benefit of Residents Pedestrians and Cyclists*, Traffic Advisory Unit Leaflet 1/87, HMSO, London.

Fleming, R. and Burrows, J. (1987) *The Case for Lighting as a Means of Preventing Crime*, Home Office Research and Planning Unit, HMSO, London.

Gottfredson, M. R. (1984) *Victims of Crime: The dimensions of risk*, Home Office Research Study No 81, HMSO, London.

Heal, and Laycock, (1987) *Preventing Juvenile Crime; the Staffordshire Experience*, Home Office, HMSO, London.

Home Office Circular (1984) *Crime Prevention*, HMSO, London.

Home Office (1988) *The Cost of Crime*, Home Standing Conference on Crime Prevention, HMSO, London.

Home Office (1988) *Practical Ways to Crack Crime*, HMSO, London.

Home Office (1988) *The Five Towns Initiative: A community reponse to offending*, HMSO, London.

Home Office Crime Prevention College (1989) *Police Architectural Liaison Manual of Guidance*, Home Office, Stafford, HMSO, London.

Hope, T. and Shaw, M. (eds) (1988) *Communities and Crime Reduction*, Home Office Research and Planning Unit, HMSO, London.

Hough, M. and Mayhew, P. (1985) *Taking Account of Crime: Key findings from the 2nd British Crime Survey*, Home Office Research Study No 85, HMSO, London.

Husain, S. (1988) *Neighbourhood Watch in England and Wales: A locational analysis*, Home Office Crime Prevention Unit, Paper No 12, Home Office, HMSO, London.

Mayhew, P., Elliott, D. and Dowds, L. (1989) *The 1988 British Crime Survey*, Home Office Research Study 111, HMSO, London.

Maxfield, M. G. (1984) *Fear of Crime in England and Wales*, Home Office Research Study No 78, HMSO, London.

Parliamentary All Party Home Affairs Committee (1985–6), *Racial Attacks and Harassment*, HC409, HMSO, London.

Power, A. (1984) *Local Housing Management*, A Priority Estates Project Survey, DoE, HMSO, London.

Power, A. (1987a) The Priority Estate Project Model, *The PEP Guide to Local Housing Management*, The Priority Estates Project, Estate Action 1 DoE/WO, HMSO, London.

Power, A. (1987b) *The PEP Experience*, The Priority Estates Project, Estate Action 2 DoE/WO, HMSO, London.

Power, A. (1987c) *Guidelines for Setting Up New Projects, The PEP Guide to Local Housing Management*, The Priority Estates Project, Estate Action 3 DoE/WO, HMSO, London.

Scottish Development Department *Housing Development: Layout, Roads and Services*, Scottish Housing Handbook, HMSO, London.

Scottish Office (1988) *The British Crime Survey, Scotland*, Scottish Office Central Research Unit, Edinburgh, HMSO, London.

Scottish Office (1989) *Criminal Statistics, Scotland*, Edinburgh, HMSO, London.

Shapland, J. (1988) Policing with the Public, in *Communities and Crime Reduction*, Home Office Research and Planning Unit, HMSO, London, pp. 116–25.

Skilton, M. (1988) *A Better Reception*, Department of the Environment Estate Action Group, HMSO, London.

Smith, L. (1988) *Domestic Violence: An overview of the literature*, Home Office Research Study 107, HMSO, London.

Walmsley, R. (1986) *Personal Violence*, Home Office Research Study No 89, HMSO, London.

Walmsley, R. and Smith, L. (eds) (1982) *Home Office Research Bulletin No 13*, Home Office Research and Planning Unit, HMSO, London.

Winchester, S. and Jackson, H. (1982) *Residential Burglary: The limits of prevention*, Home Office Research Study No 74, HMSO, London.

Women's National Commission (1985) *Violence Against Women*, Cabinet Office, HMSO, London.

PUBLICATIONS FROM THE SAFE NEIGHBOURHOODS UNIT

All of the publications below are available from: The Safe Neighbour-hoods Unit, 1st Floor, 485–487 Bethnal Green Road, London E2 9QH.

Bright, J. *et al.* (1985) *After Entry Phones: Improving management and security in multi-storey Blocks*, NACRO Safe Neighbourhoods Unit.

Crouch, S. (1989) *Practical Guide to Improving Timber Entrance Door Security*, Safe Neighbourhoods Advisory Service.

Crouch, S. (1989) *Practical Guide to Improving Window Security*, Safe Neighbourhoods Advisory Service.

Crouch, S. (1989) *Practical Guide to Improved Fixing Methods*, Safe Neighbourhoods Advisory Service.

Crouch, S. (1989) *Practical Guide to Improving Emergency Exit Door Security*, Safe Neighbourhoods Advisory Service.

Crouch, S. (1990) *Practical Guide to Improving Doors to Flats in Multi-storey Blocks*, Safe Neighbourhoods Advisory Service.

Crouch, S. (1990) *Practical Guide to Improving the Security of Flat Conversions*, Safe Neighbourhoods Advisory Service.

National Safe Neighbourhoods (1988) *Policing Housing Estates*, NACRO Crime Prevention Advisory Committee.

National Safe Neighbourhoods (1989) *Growing Up on Housing Estates: A review of play and youth provision*, NACRO Crime Prevention Advisory Committee.

Osborn, S. (1989) *Safe Communities 1989: Local government action on crime prevention and community safety*, Safe Neighbourhoods Advisory Service.

Osborn, S. and Bright, J. (1989) *Crime Prevention and Community Safety: A practical guide for local authorities*, National Safe Neighbourhoods, NACRO.

Safe Neighbourhoods Unit (1985) *Clapton Park Estate Progress Report: Part One*.

Safe Neighbourhoods Unit (1986) *The Safe Neighbourhoods Unit: A report on the Unit's work 1981–1986*.

Safe Neighbourhoods Unit (1987) *Crime and Safety on Lansdowne Green Estate*.

Safe Neighbourhoods Unit (1987) *Coming Home to Trellick: Proposals for Improving Management and security in an inner city tower block*.

Safe Neighbourhoods Unit (1988) *Beyond the Barrier: Improving management and security on Southwyck House, Brixton*.

Safe Neighbourhoods Unit (1989) *Barbot Street Estate Tower Blocks: Survey into improvements of tower block security*.

Safe Neighbourhoods Unit (1989) *Lighting Up Brent: Survey into lighting and safety on Chalk Hill, Stonebridge and South Kilburn Estates.*

Safe Neighbourhoods Unit (1989) *The Mozart Survey, Part One: A study of design modifications and housing management.*

Safe Neighbourhoods Unit (1989) *The Castle Green Estate Project Report: Survey into improvements of tower block security.*

Safe Neighbourhoods Unit (1989) *The East Spitalfields Report: Survey on management and security in East Spitalfields.*

Safe Neighbourhoods Unit (1989) *The Milton Court Report: Survey into security and management on the Milton Court Estate, Deptford.*

PAMPHLETS AND REPORTS

Bailey, G. (1987) *New Life for Old Estates: Management options for council housing reviewed*, Conservative Political Centre, London.

Bennett, G., Noble, J. and Jenks, M. (1987) *Roads and Parking in Private Sector Housing Schemes*, Housing Research Foundation.

Bennett, T. (1987) *An Evaluation of Two Neighbourhood Watch Schemes in London*, Institute of Criminology, University of Cambridge, Cambridge.

Bonnerjea, L. and Lawton, J. (1988) *No Racial Harassment This Week*, Policy Studies Unit,

Commission for Racial Equality (1987) *Living in Terror: A report on racial violence and harassment in housing*, CRE, London.

Donnison, D. *et al.* (1986) *Neighbourhood Watch: Policing the people*, Police Foundation,

Electricity Council (1987) *Essentials of Security Lighting*,

Forbes, D. (1988) *Action on Racial Harassment: Legal remedies and local authorities*, Legal Action Group and London Housing Unit,

Gardiner, R. A. (1978) *Design for Safe Neighbourhoods: The environment planning and design process*, A United States Government Information Product,

Gateshead Metropolitan Borough Council (1988) *Safer by Design*, Crime Prevention Policy Document, Gateshead Borough Council, Gateshead.

Hoggart, P. and Hambleton, R. (1987) *Decentralisation and Democracy: Localising public services*, School of Advanced Urban Studies, Bristol.

Kinsey, R. (1984) *Merseyside Crime Survey First Report: Liverpool*, Merseyside County Council, Liverpool.

Lea, J., Mathews, R. and Young, J. (1987) *Law and Order Five Years On*, Middlesex Polytechnic, London.

Lea, J. *et al.* (1988) *Preventing Crime – the Hilldrop Environmental Improvement Survey*, Middlesex Polytechnic.

Levison, D. and Atkins, J. (1987) *The Key to Equality: The 1986 Women and Housing Survey*, Institute of Housing, Women in Housing Working Party, London.

Local Authorities Housing and Racial Equality Working Party (1987) *Racial Harassment*, Association of Metropolitan Authorities,

London Planning Aid Service (1987) *Planning for Women*, Research Paper 3, London Planning Service, London.

London Strategic Policy Unit (1988) *Women's Safe Transport in London*, LSPU Transport Group, London.

Manchester City Council (1987) *Planning a Safer Environment*, Report on the Planning for Women Group, Manchester City Council, Manchester.

Middlesex Polytechnic (1990) *The Second Islington Crime Survey, Centre for Criminology*, Middlesex Polytechnic, London.

Mount, B. (1988) *Putting Research into Practise*, a paper presented to the London Road Safety Committee Seminar.

National Council for Civil Liberties (1989) *Who's Watching You? Surveillance in Public Places*, Liberty Briefing No 16, NCCC, London.

National House-Building Council (NHBC) (1986) *Guidance on how the Security of New Homes can be Improved*, NHBC,

Newman, O. (1980) *Community of Interest*, Anchor Press/Double Day, New York.

Nwagbajo, and Carter, (1985) *A Study of Victim Support*, London Borough of Hackney Community Psychiatry Research Unit, London.

Pettersen, G. (1988) *Community Safety in Camden: an independent study*, London Borough of Camden, London.

Poyner, B., Helson, P. and Webb, P. (1985) *Layout of Residential Areas and its Influence on Crime*, Tavistock Institute of Human Relations, London.

Poyner, B. and Webb, B. (1986) *Crime Reduction on Housing Estates: An evaluation of NACRO's Crime Prevention Programme*, The Tavistock Institute of Public Relations, London.

Poyner, B. (1987) *Design and Security in Public Open Spaces*, Tavistock Institute of Human Relations, London.

Southwark Council (1985) *Housing Security Design Guide*, Planning Department, Southwark Borough Council, London.

Tomaney, J. (1987) *Crime, Security and Council Housing: A review of some current crime prevention and community safety practice by London Boroughs*, London Research Centre Housing Group, London.

Watkins Gray International (UK), *Building Design for Security – A Review*, Buildings Research Establishment, Department of the Environment, London.

Ware, V. (1988) *Women's Safety on Housing Estates*, Women's Design Service, London.

JOURNAL ARTICLES

Adams, J. (1973) *DRS Journal: Design Research and Methods*, **7** (3), 266–7.

Allatt, P. (1984) Residential security: Containment and displacement of burglary, *Howard Journal of Penology and Criminology*, **23** (2), 99–116.

Allatt, P. (1984) Fear of crime: The effect of improved residential security on a difficult to let estate, *Howard Journal of Penology and Criminology*, **23** (4), 170–82.

Anson, B. (1986) Removing walkways is not nearly enough, *Town and Country Planning*, **55** (6), 174–5.

Bacon, C. (1985) Deck access housing, *Housing Planning Review*, **40** (2), 18–21.

Bone, S. (1986) Security: Architectural ironmongery, *Architect*, **93** (12), 55–62.

Burian, P. (1987) Lighting for security, *Building Design*, 3 April, p 23.

Clarke, R. *et al.* (1985) Elderly victims of crime and exposure to risk, *Howard Journal of Criminal Justice*, **24,** (1), 1–9.

Coleman, A. (1985) Reducing estate crime figures with design improvement schemes, *Municipal Journal*, **93** (25), 1044–6.

Coleman, A. (1986) Design improvement: Utopia goes on trial, *Town and Country Planning*, **55,** (5), 138–40.

Coleman, A. (1986) Dangerous dreams, *Landscape Design*, (163), 29–31.

Coleman, A. (1987) More sensitive housing – Design criteria please, *House Builder*, 23–6.

Cowan, R. (1988) Prevention but no cure, *Architects' Journal*, **187** (1), 32–9.

Dawson, G. and Parker, J. (1986) Need for guidelines to tackle local crime, *Town and Country Planning*, **55** (5), 141–4.

Farringdon *et al.* (1986) Unemployment, school leaving and crime, *British Journal of Criminology*, **26** (4),

Hellman, L. (1988) Paradise regained – Housing renewal, Wirral, *Architects Journal*, **187** (31), 33–47.

Hillier, B. (1986) City of Alice's Dreams, *Architects' Journal*, **184** (28), 39–41.

Jackson, V. (1982) Who is Designing for Whom, *Housing*, **18** (10), 18–19.

Jones, G. M. (1987) Elderly people and domestic crime: Reflections on ageism, sexism and victimology, *British Journal of Criminology*, **27** (2), 191–201.

National Association for the Care and Rehabilitation of Offenders (NACRO) (1974) Architecture, planning and urban crime 7804, *Surveyor*, **107**, 28–29.

Ormerod R. (1984) Design and policing, *Housing Planning Review*, **39** (6), 18–19.

Shapland, J. and Vagg, J. (1987) Using the Police, *British Journal of Criminology*, **27** (1), 54–63.

Smith, S. J. (1987) Design against crime? Beyond the rhetoric of residential crime prevention, *Property Management*, **5** (2), 146–150.

Stollard, P. J. (1984) The architecture of no-mans land, *Architects Journal*, **180** (31), 24–41.

Taylor, K. (1988) Burglars get access over the garden wall, *British Journal of Criminology*, **28** (3),

Underwood, G. (1986) Crime prevention and housing design, *Architect*, **93** (12), 71–73.

Williams, A. and Partners (1986) Islington houses, *Building*, **251** (34), 37–42.

Wilson, P. (1984/85) Crime prevention: The community approach, *House Builder*, 40–41.